FEMINIST THEORIES *for* DRAMATIC CRITICISM

GAYLE AUSTIN

THE UNIVERSITY OF MICHIGAN PRESS
Ann Arbor

Library of Congress Cataloging-in-Publication Data

Austin, Gayle, 1949–
    Feminist theories for dramatic criticism / Gayle Austin.
      p. cm.
    Includes bibliographical references and index.
    ISBN 0-472-09429-7 (cloth : alk.). — ISBN 0-472-06429-0 (paper :
alk.)
    1. Drama—History and criticism—Theory, etc.   2. Feminist
criticism.   3. American drama—History and criticism—Theory, etc.
I. Title.
PN1633.F45A9   1990
801'.952'082—dc20   90-45986

To the women who raised me:
my mother, Ethel Woolson Austin Dempsey,
and my aunts, Myrtle Woolson Eley
and Elizabeth Woolson Murrin

Acknowledgments

Many women writing today about feminism and/or theater have helped me with the writing of this book. Sue-Ellen Case in 1984 gave me a germinal bibliography and the belief that theory, feminism, and theater could mix. Jill Dolan has been a supportive and constructive reader of this work as it has evolved and I want to acknowledge her help in my thinking through many ideas of feminism and representation. Among those who have read parts of the manuscript and given valuable criticism, I especially want to thank Elinor Fuchs, Milly Barranger, Kay Beck, and Valerie Fennell. I also want to acknowledge the inspiration given to me by many members of the Women and Theatre Program of the Association for Theatre in Higher Education, particularly Elin Diamond.

I especially thank Julia Miles, who got me into all this to begin with, and the playwrights and directors of the Women's Project, who have helped keep me going. A grant from Sallie Bingham and the Kentucky Foundation for Women gave me encouragement and time, both of which have enriched this book. LeAnn Fields at University of Michigan Press has been a staunch supporter throughout the long period of revision and preparation of the manuscript.

I would also like to thank my mentors at the City University of New York Graduate Center—Marvin Carlson, Vera M. Roberts, Albert Bermel, Mary Ann Caws, and Margaret Knapp—as well as my colleagues at Georgia State University in Atlanta.

Most thanks to Natalie Zdanow, for her patience, supportiveness, and quiet confidence that I could do it.

Contents

CHAPTER 1

Feminist Theories:
Paying Attention to Women

Why This Book? And How?

One of the most famous lines in American drama is "So attention must be paid." Linda Loman was referring to her husband, Willy, in Arthur Miller's *Death of a Salesman*. He was a human being and he was in trouble. The problem for Linda, and for women, is that the entire play paid attention to Willy and his trouble. In 1949 no one even asked, "But what about Linda?" Forty years later feminist critics are asking many questions: Is Linda a stereotype of wife and mother? If so, what damage does that image do? What women playwrights were writing in 1949 and how do their plays differ from Miller's? Is Linda a male construct of an idealized "Woman" who reinforces the desires of the dominant ideology in this culture? What problems are caused by such a play being taken as "realistic"? Should plays like this be deconstructed in production in order to demonstrate the mechanisms by which they manipulate the audience?

A feminist approach to anything means paying attention to women. It means paying attention when women appear as characters and noticing when they do not. It means making some "invisible" mechanisms visible and pointing out, when necessary, that while the emperor has no clothes, the empress has no body. It means paying attention to women as writers and as readers or audience members. It means taking nothing for granted because the things we take for granted are usually those that were constructed from the most powerful point of view in the culture and that is not the point of view of women.

Feminist theories have been produced in many fields of study, particularly in the last twenty years. The field of dramatic criticism has been relatively slow to acknowledge this work and to incorporate it. One of my purposes in this book is to demonstrate the usefulness as critical tools for the analysis of drama of feminist theories from four fields of study: literary criticism, anthropology, psychology, and film theory. Of course, these theories can and should be combined for a full feminist analysis of most works, but for the sake of clarity I will deal with each field separately. My purpose is not to develop a monolithic theory of feminist dramatic criticism. I would rather err on the side of presenting too many theories than advocate any single approach. I would call mine a selective pluralism, based on a combination of pragmatism and personal preferences.

Another purpose is to demonstrate that drama, not to mention the entire realm of live performance, has barely been tapped as a source of material by the field of women's studies. Women comfortable with the idea of interdisciplinary work still shy away from using dramatic texts, preferring to draw theories from and analyze prose, poetry, or film texts. Post–World War II American drama is particularly ripe for analysis using postwar feminist theory. Yet the two have so far very rarely intersected.

Drama presents several problems as an object of study. It is more difficult than fiction or poetry to read on the page. Live performances of it are temporal, yet, unlike films and video, not convenient to study in detail. The writing of plays requires mastering to some degree a male-dominated, public production machinery, something that relatively few women have been able to do over the long history of the form, and consequently there is not as large a body of extant plays by women as there is of novels. Only a handful of plays by women have entered the canon of "approved" works that are published, anthologized, taught, and produced, so that we are not used to associating women with playwriting.

But despite these difficulties, there are advantages for the feminist critical project of studying plays. Plays allow the reader and audience to visualize, to fill in blanks and gaps. They provide the frameworks for productions that can bring out many of the issues feminism finds pressing. They combine verbal and nonverbal elements simultaneously, so that questions of language and visual representation can be addressed at the same time, through the medium of an actual body. They contribute a unique field of examples of women's representation.

My purposes in writing this book have their roots in my history. My earliest experience of consciousness of the intersection of women and theater came from working as literary manager of The Women's Project at the American Place Theatre in New York City from 1978 to 1984. I read hundreds of new plays written by American women and helped administer 130 staged readings and 26 productions of them. The aim of this still ongoing project is to help more women move into the mainstream of playwriting and directing.

My interest in feminist theory was clarified and developed while doing doctoral research at the City University of New York Graduate Center. In 1983 there was almost no feminist dramatic theory published, but the theory I found in other fields seemed very applicable to drama. During my graduate school years (1983–87) and the years since, the field of feminist dramatic criticism has expanded, with journal issues and entire books now devoted to feminist theory and theater. My personal journey has taken me from the simple desire to see more female images on the stage and move more women into the mainstream of American theater, to a particular interest in women's playwriting, to a passion about the much broader issue of how drama and theater operate to represent women on the stage. In a political sense, I have moved from the position of liberal feminist to that of radical and then materialist feminist (these types of feminism are discussed further on in this chapter).

In this book I stress drama rather than performance because ever since I began to work in developing new plays, I have been fascinated by the written text that remains after performance is forgotten. It is what "becomes" of the play, what the play "means" to succeeding generations, the means for teaching and producing the play after its original production. At the same time it is only a blueprint for what the performance can be. It is an open form too often, in history, closed to women.

I draw on contemporary American drama because it is the most accessible body of texts to a majority of American theater practitioners and is also the most available (in print as well as performance) to scholars in all fields. All the plays analyzed were first produced in the United States after World War II. Playwrights include prominent figures in the traditional canon (Eugene O'Neill, Arthur Miller, Lillian Hellman, Sam Shepard),

3

as well as some women playwrights who would not generally be placed there (Jane Bowles, Alice Childress). The plays selected bring up particularly interesting issues of gender.

This book consists of my readings of existing theories and applications of them to specific plays. I use theories to develop new interpretations of plays, not new theories. The theories have been selected from those developed in four fields of study since the latest wave of feminist scholarship began (approximately in 1970) by writers who identify themselves as feminist. Selection from within this group was based on the influence of the theorist and the value I found her ideas to have when applied to drama.

In this chapter I will introduce some of the general ideas about feminist theory that I will use throughout the book: the three political divisions of feminism, contributions of black and lesbian feminist criticism to the overall project of feminist theory, and three stages of feminist criticism that have been outlined in literary criticism and other fields. Each of the four central chapters deals with one field of study and the feminist theory it has developed, focusing on one theorist and applying her ideas to one or two plays. The aim is not to say how "good" or "bad" the plays are from the point of view of feminism, but to show how using a feminist theory can illuminate the plays. Each chapter will sample the possibilities for analyzing drama but is not intended as a final feminist reading of the play. The last chapter will point toward some possible future work in the field.

Political Feminisms

One of the most basic issues in working with feminist theory is defining the various political types of feminism and making one's own preference clear at the onset of critical work. Fortunately, there are now several formulations of the political feminisms. But before outlining them, I want to express a note of caution about making categories too important. In compensating for a past in which political biases were generally not clearly expressed and therefore "invisible," there is a danger of creating a present in which political lines are too clearly drawn. There may be a tendency to pressure each individual to "take sides" in order to be clear, and we may lose something in the process.

One of the things that might be lost is the ability to work from a liminal critical perspective—that is, one that falls between more clearly defined positions (see beginning of chap. 3). The position I most often take myself these days is of "woman in the cracks" between major categories. We may lose the liminal drama that does not seem to be easily analyzed from any one position. The women who wrote those plays might have been "in the cracks" themselves. I have reached the provisional conclusion that this may be the most fruitful position for a theorist or a practitioner to take.

In their recent, ground-breaking books Sue-Ellen Case and Jill Dolan have discussed various political divisions of feminisms in relation to theater.[1] Using the work of Alison Jaggar,[2] Dolan describes three main divisions: liberal, cultural, and materialist. Liberal feminism developed from liberal humanism, stressing women's parity with men, based on "universal" values. Dolan examines the Broadway reception of Marsha Norman's *'night, Mother* in terms of "the traditional critical search for universality and transcendance [sic]" and "the issue of canon formation" (5). She uses the term *cultural feminism* to describe the form that "bases its analysis in a reification of sexual difference based on absolute gender categories" (5). Cultural feminists stress that women are both different from and superior to men and often advocate expressing this fact through female forms of culture. Jaggar and Case use the term *radical* for this second form of feminism. I have also chosen that term, based on its more political connotations. The radical feminist point of view frequently addresses the question of a "female aesthetic" as well as the desirability of a separate female culture. It is criticized, however, for being essentialist, or using as a basic premise that there is an absolute "essence" of "Woman" and the most important difference between women and men is their biological makeup. Many critics have discussed the difficulties for women inherent in essentialism.[3]

Of the three feminisms, both Dolan and Case prefer to adopt a materialist position, which Dolan says "deconstructs the mythic subject Woman to look at women as a class oppressed by material conditions and social relations" (10). Both devote chapters in their books to radical (or cultural) and materialist feminism. These chapters give an excellent introduction to the implications of these two types of feminism for theater. One major advantage of a materialist approach is the prominent position given to questions of race, class, and sexual preference, which receive little treatment in either liberal or radical feminism.[4]

Liberal feminism, which is given the shortest treatment of the three

5

by Dolan and Case, seems until now to have been used mostly in getting more women employed in certain fields of theater and in forming certain groups, such as The Women's Project and the original Women's Program of the American Theatre Association. The use of liberal feminism as a critical tool has not been explored. In Case and Dolan the emphasis is on materialist analysis, with occasional use of a radical idea. I have come to see the enormous usefulness of the materialist feminism, though I do think that more critical use needs to be made of liberal and radical feminism in theater.

In brief, my own summaries of the three divisions are:

Liberal
  1. Minimizes differences between men and women
  2. Works for success within system; reform, not revolt
  3. Individual more important than the group

Radical
  1. Stresses superiority of female attributes and difference between male and female modes
  2. Favors separate female systems
  3. Individual more important than the group

Materialist
  1. Minimizes biological differences between men and women
  2. Stresses material conditions of production such as history, race, class, gender
  3. Group more important than the individual

Black Feminist Criticism

Commitment to a materialist feminist approach makes it imperative that other categories of oppression be considered along with that of gender. Analysis of race, class, and sexual preference gives additional dimensions to feminist criticism and moves a critic away from the white, middle-class, heterosexual "norms" that are often presumed without comment. The positions of women of color are particularly some to which "attention must be paid." Yet, as Sue-Ellen Case points out, doing this is sometimes problematic for a white feminist such as myself:

Because this description of the position and project of women of colour has been written by a white author, the discourse is necessarily distanced from the actual experiences which shape this position. The distance is not an objective distance, but one which reflects a perspective of racial and class privilege. . . . Moreover, within the study of feminism and theatre, this distance creates crucial problems in research and criticism. Many of the materials on ethnic feminist theatre practice and writing are difficult to obtain, which reflects the alternative nature of the project.[5]

The largest available body of feminist work related to the writings of women of color concerns black women. Many of the issues surrounding black feminist criticism have been raised in a series of essays in the field of literary criticism. One of the earliest and most influential is "Toward a Black Feminist Criticism" by Barbara Smith. First published in 1977, it was reprinted in two white-edited feminist criticism anthologies and prompted many responses. In it Smith not only pointed out the need for a black feminist critical perspective, but also called for recognition of the black lesbian perspective. She pointed out ways in which white male, black male, and white female critics either misinterpreted or made invisible writing by black women, and asked "to see in print white women's acknowledgment of the contradictions of who and what are being left out of their research and writing."[6] She outlined a few principles that a black feminist critic might use: "a primary commitment to exploring how both sexual and racial politics and Black and female identity are inextricable elements in Black women's writings"; "the assumption that Black women writers constitute an identifiable literary tradition"; examination of "traditional Black female activities of rootworking, herbal medicine, conjure, and midwifery" and "Black female language"; and critical insights drawn first from black women rather than trying to "graft the ideas or methodology of white/male literary thought upon the precious materials of Black women's art" (174–75).

Smith used a black lesbian feminist approach to examine Toni Morrison's novel *Sula,* and ended her essay by calling for "one book based in Black feminist and Black lesbian experience, fiction or nonfiction. Just one work to reflect the reality that I and the Black women whom I love are trying to create" (184). Her call was answered within a few years when

Alice Walker's *The Color Purple* was published. A similar call for a black lesbian feminist play may still be unanswered.

Among the women responding to Smith's essay was Deborah McDowell. In a 1980 essay she criticized Smith's definition of "lesbian" as imprecise, agreed with other elements, and then gave her own definition of black feminist criticism:

> I use the term here simply to refer to Black female critics who analyze the works of Black female writers from a feminist or political perspective. But the term can also apply to any criticism written by a Black woman regardless of her subject or perspective—a book written by a male from a feminist or political perspective, a book written by a Black woman or about Black women authors in general, or any writings by women.[7]

She advocates both contextual criticism, taking into account the influence of black history and culture on literature, and textual analysis, which would include tracing common themes such as "the thwarted female artist," "clothing as iconography," and "the Black female's journey." She also advocates drawing on feminist scholarship in other disciplines and examining the work of black male writers beyond negative images of black women (192–96).

These two essays laid out many of the issues of black feminist criticism that continued to be debated through the 1980s.[8] By 1989, in an anthology edited by Elaine Showalter, Valerie Smith addressed herself to feminists' insertion of gender into the main body of Afro-Americanist literary criticism. The move from addressing women's works and issues to addressing the entire issue of "gender" has in itself been controversial, with some feminists seeing it as assimilation that saps energy and diverts attention from the political issues specific to women. But within the context of gender, Valerie Smith finds that black feminist critics "call attention to the masculinist assumptions of the canon"; "expanded and diversified the body of texts taught by and written about by members of the scholarly community"; "complicate received ideas about the contours of the Afro-American tradition by exploring suppressed rituals, conventions, and narrative strategies in the writings of black women"; and "theorize the interconnections among cultural constructions of race, class, *and* gender in both the language and the ideological assumptions of black texts."[9]

The debates about definitions and methodologies in the field have very rarely taken into account black women playwrights. Some criticism of individual plays and playwrights has been done by both white and black critics, both female and male. But the work that can most clearly be seen as the counterpart of black feminist criticism in the literary field has been done by black women theater scholars in the form of history, biography or biographical criticism, personal testimony, and two anthologies of plays with introductions.[10] More often than not this work has not been identified by its authors as feminist, and there is an almost total absence of feminist theory in the work.

The Question of Theory

Approaches to developing black feminist theory, some aspects of which might be applicable to drama, have begun in fields such as politics and sociology. Some work has involved the concepts of the margin, black feminist ideology based on the "double jeopardy" of race and sex, and a theory of knowledge based on black women's standpoint.[11]

The use of theory in black feminist criticism has been called into question by Barbara Christian in her essay "The Race for Theory." She considers Western literary theory elitist, apolitical, and not relevant to the black feminist project of giving exposure to black women writers who have been disvalued in white culture. She points out that "people of color have always theorized—but in forms quite different from the Western form of abstract logic. . . . often in narrative forms."[12] She finds white feminist literary theories objectionable for many reasons: they "restrict the definition of what *feminist* means and overgeneralize"; they don't take into account "that women are of many races and ethnic backgrounds with different histories and cultures . . . different classes that have different concerns"; and that they often "acknowledge that women of color, for example, do exist, then go on to do what they were going to do anyway, which is to invent a theory that has little relevance for us" (75). This scathing indictment makes the project of including black women in feminist theorizing seem difficult indeed. Perhaps all white feminists can do at this time is "acknowledge" and "go on to do what they were going to do anyway," with the hope that their theories will eventually broaden and become useful for black feminists as well.

On the question of theory itself, black feminist critics are not the only ones with reservations. Among white feminist literary critics, for example, while Jane Marcus favors the move toward theory in her influential essay "Storming the Toolshed,"[13] Nina Baym argues that theory merely "addresses an audience of prestigious male academics and attempts to win its respect." Laurie Finke counters in a later issue of *Tulsa Studies in Women's Literature* that Baym and others against theory are in actuality using a theory (structuralism) without acknowledging it.[14]

Among many other formulations of what feminist theory is or could be is Elizabeth Meese's, which draws on the literary theory field of deconstruction and moves on to say: "To refuse to theorize could in itself be to create a theory . . . in the form of continual, conscious 'de-centering' instead of being silenced or seeking an 'equal' voice. . . . From this perspective, there will never be *a theory* of feminist criticism; rather, feminist criticism will be a theorizing process. . . ."[15] Another, more essentialist approach is taken by Ruth Salvaggio, who combines ideas from film and from psychoanalytic and French feminist theorists to posit three spaces within which feminists might theorize: "the marginal space, the space of the body, and liquid space."[16]

While the warnings of feminist anti-theorists should be noted, they need not stop development. I hope this book will help broaden the perception of what theory is, particularly feminist theory: where it can come from, what it can do, how it may or may not take a different form from male-developed theory. I hope it will help make theory more accessible to those who may be theory-shy for any reason, ranging from dread of jargon to thinking it useless in the "real world."

For me, theory is a way of thinking. It means stepping back from the myriad details of theater production to take a broader view: What are we producing, what is it saying about women, and is that what we want it to be saying? It means stepping back from day-to-day teaching and asking: What are we teaching, what are the plays saying to students about women, and what are other possible messages? It means seeing that practitioners can be theorists and theorists can be practitioners, and asking what they can learn from each other. Theory is a text, to be read in a variety of ways like any other. It could even serve as a dramatic text. What would a "theory play" look like? These questions can only begin to be addressed if feminist theater critics and practitioners grab onto theory and try to use it.

Lesbian Feminist Criticism

Several white lesbian feminist critics in theater are exploring a wide range of radical and materialist theory. Jill Dolan addresses herself to Barbara Christian's objections to theory in a recent article. While Christian says, "What I write and how I write is done in order to save my own life" (77), Dolan responds, "I work in theory to save mine. Theory allows me to articulate my differences from a feminism I first learned as monolithic." She can locate her identity "in the conflicting discourses of lesbianism and Judaism, and know that there is no comfortable place for me within any single discourse."[17] Part of the value of lesbian feminist theory and criticism is to point out, as black feminist theory does, that there is no single "Woman" position that encompasses all women, though the white, middle-class, heterosexual model is the one established by the dominant powers in this culture.

Like black feminist criticism, lesbian feminist criticism by its very existence can question this model and make visible the way it has been constructed. The black lesbian position is probably the one from which this criticism can most clearly be spoken, but there are relatively few critics working from that position. As Barbara Smith has pointed out, "Heterosexual privilege is usually the only privilege that Black women have. None of us have racial or sexual privilege, almost none of us have class privilege; maintaining 'straightness' is our last resort." She goes on to comment on the homophobia in the black community: "A community which has not confronted sexism, because a widespread Black feminist movement has not required it to, has likewise not been challenged to examine its heterosexism. Even at this moment I am not convinced that one can write explicitly as a Black lesbian and live to tell about it" (182).

Bonnie Zimmerman's widely anthologized article "What Has Never Been: An Overview of Lesbian Feminist Criticism" serves as an introduction to many of the ideas and possibilities for drama criticism raised by lesbian critics. She describes heterosexism in feminist criticism, talks about definitions of "lesbian," points out various critical approaches, and mentions some uses of a lesbian perspective. She says, "Heterosexism is the set of values and structures that assumes heterosexuality to be the only natural form of sexual and emotional expression." Under almost all lesbian criticism is the assumption:

that a woman's identity is not defined only by her relation to a male world and male literary tradition . . . , that powerful bonds between women are a crucial factor in women's lives, and that the sexual and emotional orientation of a woman profoundly affects her consciousness and thus her creativity.[18]

One potentially useful concept outlined by Zimmerman is that "woman-identified writers, silenced by a homophobic and misogynistic society, have been forced to adopt coded and obscure language and internal censorship" (186). This applies not only to overtly lesbian writers, such as Gertrude Stein, but also to a wide range of "woman-identified" writers, such as Emily Dickinson, Angelina Weld Grimke, Mary Wollstonecraft, and Sarah Orne Jewett. In the field of playwriting there are many such women whose work could benefit from decoding.

Within lesbian criticism there is a marked difference between radical and materialist perspectives. One of the most important theorists for radical lesbian feminist criticism is the poet Adrienne Rich. She has written a number of theoretical essays, but one, "Compulsory Heterosexuality and Lesbian Existence," has been widely read, cited, and debated since its publication in 1980. In it she had two main concerns:

first, how and why women's choice of women as passionate comrades, life partners, co-workers, lovers, tribe, has been crushed, invalidated, forced into hiding and disguise; and second, the virtual or total neglect of lesbian existence in a wide range of writings, including feminist scholarship.[19]

In exploring those concerns she raised a host of issues, among them that "the assumption that 'most women are innately heterosexual' stands as a theoretical and political stumbling block for many women," and that "the failure to examine heterosexuality as an institution is like failing to admit that the economic system called capitalism or the caste system of racism is maintained by a variety of forces, including both physical violence and false consciousness" (648).

A Rich concept particularly helpful to criticism is that of the lesbian continuum. By this she means "a range—through each woman's life and throughout history—of woman-identified experience." This would include not just genital sexual experience but "the sharing of a rich inner life, the bonding against male tyranny, the giving and receiving of practical and political support." The erotic would be defined in female terms "as that which is unconfined to any single part of the body or solely to the body itself, as an energy not only diffuse but . . . omnipresent." She suggests:

> If we consider the possibility that all women—from the infant suckling her mother's breast, to the grown woman experiencing orgasmic sensations while suckling her own child, perhaps recalling her mother's milk-smell in her own . . . to the woman dying at ninety, touched and handled by women—exist on a lesbian continuum, we can see ourselves as moving in and out of this continuum, whether we identify ourselves as lesbian or not. (648–51)

Several women responded to Rich's formulations. Ann Ferguson found that "her position contains serious flaws from a socialist-feminist perspective" and presented "a different, historically linked concept of lesbian identity." Her main objection was that Rich's model "does not allow us to understand the collective and social nature of a lesbian identity as opposed to lesbian practices or behaviors."[20] Jacquelyn Zita, on the other hand, argued against Ferguson's view, suggesting that "there are several good reasons for adopting the idea of a lesbian continuum as a strategic term. . . . One problem I have always had with socialist-feminist theory," writes Zita, "is its tendency to obscure and occlude an understanding of how central the institution of heterosexuality is to our womanly existences."[21] As a radical feminist, she agreed with Rich's patriarchal, rather than just social, critique.

Zimmerman asks several questions that might be applied to dramatic criticism:

> How, for example, does the lesbian's sense of outlaw status affect her literary vision? Might lesbian writing, because of the lesbian's position on the boundaries, be characterized by a particular sense of freedom and flexibility or, rather, by images of violently imposed barriers, the closet? Or, in fact, is there a dialectic between freedom and imprisonment that is unique to lesbian writing? (202)

She also suggests we might ask "how lesbianism functions as a sign within the text," and offers French novelist Monique Wittig as one who "locates the lesbian subject outside the male linguistic universe" (195). Wittig is also a theorist whose writings may be useful in dramatic criticism. Her work is basically materialist and stresses in several articles Simone de Beauvoir's idea that "one is not born, but becomes a woman."[22] In a 1988 article, Marilyn Farwell discusses various definitions of what she calls "the lesbian as metaphor," concentrating on Rich and Wittig.[23]

Dramatic criticism has produced even less work with a lesbian perspective than literary criticism has. There are a few exceptions. One book has been published discussing lesbian and male homosexual characters in plays seen on the New York stage from the 1920s to the 1950s.[24] Rosemary Curb has applied a radical lesbian perspective to plays written by women. She uses "woman-conscious drama" to mean "all drama by and about women that is characterized by multiple interior reflections of women's lives and perceptions. [It] ... may be called feminist, lesbian, lesbian/feminist, or post-modern, or it may eschew labels."[25]

A materialist approach to lesbianism has been used by several theorists who incorporate film theory (see chap. 5) in developing a concept of the lesbian subject position for theater. Jill Dolan has published a number of articles on the subject.[26] Chapter 4 of her book gives a basic introduction, defining terms and pointing out the position's usefulness for performance analysis:

> Sexuality is at base the expression of affectional preference, while gender is based on sex-class. But sexuality, in Western Culture, is as rigidly constructed and prescribed as gender. While it is crucial not to conflate sexuality with gender, expressions of sexuality further illustrate the operation of gender codes and constructs in the presentation of the female body.
>   ... Recasting sexuality as a choice—for instance shifting a woman's desire from men to other women—also affects how she sees herself as a woman. Once heterosexuality is no longer compulsory, femininity also becomes suspect as a "natural" construct.[27]

Other important materialist theorizing on the lesbian subject has been done in the late 1980s by Kate Davy, Teresa de Lauretis, and Sue-Ellen Case.[28]

Stages of Feminist Criticism

Feminist criticism has been usefully classified by chronological divisions. Several writers have divided the criticism that began around 1970 into three successive phases. But this division into periods requires some examination, for American feminist historians have made many interesting contributions to our understanding of periodization.

In 1974 Gerda Lerner delivered a paper that, revised and published several times, ended up as a chapter in her 1979 book *The Majority Finds Its Past*. In it she outlines three stages in the discipline of feminist history. For the first stage she uses the term *compensatory history* to denote work on "notable women" and *contribution history* to denote work on women's contributions to movements in male-written history. These writings, she says, "have applied questions from traditional history to women, and tried to fit women's past into the empty spaces of historical scholarship."[29] In the second stage historians have "begun to ask about the actual *experience* of women in the past," which "leads one to the use of women's letters, diaries, autobiographies, and oral history sources" (153). In the third stage, the field has "presented a challenge to some basic assumptions historians make" (154). The dividing of history into periods, for instance, has been largely based on politics and the military, two fields in which women have traditionally held little power.

A classic example of a feminist historian calling for a reconsideration of the periodization of history is an essay by Joan Kelly, "Did Women Have a Renaissance?" Her answer to this question is that "there was no renaissance for women—at least, not during the Renaissance."[30] This extreme idea, first worked out by her in 1972–73, then published in 1977 and republished in a book of her essays in 1984, has come to seem less extreme and has gained wider acceptance over the years. It is an example of third-stage feminism that questions the basic assumptions of an entire discipline. It is with caution that I approach anyone's outline of the history of feminist criticism. But the three stages provide a convenient way of referring to several predominant types of work.

Literary critic Elizabeth Abel sees the first stage as having embraced the idea of the similarity of men and women, focusing on the negative aspects of texts written by men and the limited female roles in their work. The second stage shifted to the importance of female experience and focused on the reading of texts by women, their unique qualities, and the "female tradition" of women writers. The current (1982) stage has shifted to "interrelationship as well as opposition, difference *between* as well as difference *from*," confrontation through "acts of revision, appropriation, and subversion that constitute a female text," which "translates sexual difference into literary differences of genre, structure, voice, and plot."[31]

Elaine Showalter expressed a formulation very similar to Abel's in 1985. Her third stage stresses two contributions to American theory, the English and the French, and encompasses more political considerations such as the influence of the women's movement and women's studies. For her the English have contributed "an analysis of the connection between gender and class, an emphasis on popular culture, and a feminist critique of Marxist literary theory," while the French look at "the ways that 'the feminine' has been defined, represented, or repressed in the symbolic systems of language, metaphysics, psychoanalysis, and art."[32]

A third, very interesting description of three stages of feminist theater theory and practice was outlined by Janelle Reinelt in 1989. She places the first in the late 1960s and early 1970s, during which the emphasis was on getting female characters and experience seen on stage and there was an effort to produce more plays written by women. The second, during the 1970s, was one in which "the possibilities for deconstructing gender on stage held promise for a new feminist theatre which could point out the ideological character of theatrical representation." The third stage, in the 1980s, is concerned with the "subject-as-agent," in which "the production of meaning must occur *in spite of*, or perhaps *in the face of* gender."[33] In a sense, she has combined the literary critics' stages one and two and found there to be two subsequent stages. These stages work very well for aspects of performance theory, but for purposes of analyzing drama I find the literary stages more useful.

The most concise formulation comes in the introduction to a recent book of essays on women playwrights and other theater makers. Lynda Hart states: "If the feminist writer's first efforts were investigations of the male-inscribed literary tradition, a second and ongoing effort has been to document women's realities as constructed by women writers. A shift in the last decade has been toward rigorous exploration of the language of representation itself."[34]

The stages of feminist criticism that I will apply to drama are:

1. working within the canon: examining images of women;
2. expanding the canon: focusing on women writers; and
3. exploding the canon: questioning underlying assumptions of an entire field of study, including canon formation.

Kate Millett's *Sexual Politics,* published in 1970, might be taken as the paradigm of first-stage criticism. It analyzes images of women in literature written by men, specifically the work of D. H. Lawrence, Henry Miller, and Norman Mailer. This was the book that set the pace for much of first-stage criticism in the arts. Two film books published in 1973 and 1974 also surveyed images of women: Marjorie Rosen's *Popcorn Venus* and Molly Haskell's *From Reverence to Rape*[35] were serious indictments of what the movies had made of women.

The first-stage work in dramatic criticism began much later and has not gotten as far. In 1980–81 there was a rush of work done on Shakespeare[36] that continued, along with work on other Renaissance playwrights, through the 1980s.[37] Some sporadic articles have discussed women characters in the work of an individual playwright, such as Ibsen or O'Neill, but there has been no book with the breadth or incision of Millett's or Haskell's. In the late 1980s some books have explored such first-stage topics as images of women in opera, plays by European male writers in the period 1880–1920, postwar British plays by women and men, and male-authored plays in the American canon.[38] First-stage work in some cases has been combined with stages two and three, perhaps in an effort to catch theater up to literature and film. But in comparison with those fields the groundwork, especially in contemporary American drama, is weak.

In the second stage, the focus shifted to work on women as playwrights. It began with the publication between 1973 and 1981 of a number of play anthologies.[39] The introductions and the plays themselves heightened awareness of the fact that there are American women playwrights other than Lillian Hellman and made the plays more accessible for study and production. (Many other anthologies of plays by women have been published in the last decade, including a British series called *Plays by Women* and five anthologies of plays from The Women's Project.) Then a few books addressed the question of feminist drama and the feminist theater groups of the late 1960s and early 1970s.[40] In 1982 a bibliography of the plays written by American women in this century appeared.[41] Other second-stage work on American women playwrights has been done in biography, criticism, interview, and source materials.[42] There have also been a number of articles on English-, French-, German-, and Spanish-speaking women playwrights, most working in other countries.[43] Two recent anthologies contain essays on women playwrights and groups from a variety of cultures.[44] While publication in this stage frequently incorporates a theoretical perspective, other types of stage-three work are emerging as well.

Third-stage work has been heavily materialist; it remains to be seen what shape radical and liberal feminist third-stage criticism may take. One direction stage-three theorists take is to modify some man-made tools, such as semiotics and deconstruction. The possibilities for third-stage materialist dramatic theory/criticism are already in view. The books by Case and Dolan are the clearest examples, along with Elin Diamond's article on a feminist approach to Brecht's theory and the "Feminist Diversions" issue of *Theatre Journal*.[45] Some of the topics receiving attention are feminist perspectives on traditional dramatic concerns of realism, narrative, and mimesis.[46]

Looking simultaneously at stages of feminist criticism and political divisions of feminism points up the fact that they overlap. First-stage criticism has frequently been liberal, deploring the lack of "positive" images, such as women professionals and independent women who function as actively as men. A radical feminist might call for more plays that show women functioning together in groups, while much recent materialist criticism has moved from "images" to asking whether women can be represented on the stage at all. Similarly, each political viewpoint sheds different light on second-stage work. Liberal feminists want more plays written by women to enter the canon and be produced. Radical feminists find threads of similarity among plays written by women and work on the idea of a "female aesthetic,"[47] while the "mode of production" of plays by women, including specific historical circumstances, is a materialist concern.

Much of the most recent third-stage work has appeared in the journals *Theatre Journal*, *Women & Performance*, and *TDR*, the latter two of which are based at New York University and reflect an orientation toward performance over text. An anthology of feminist articles from *Theatre Journal* in the period 1984–89 gives a good overview of the field, and a recent issue of *Women & Performance* contains an extensive bibliography of feminist dramatic criticism as well as several accounts of the history of the Women and Theatre Program of the Association for Theatre in Higher Education (ATHE).[48] Criticism of all political types is being developed, often through women talking among themselves and at academic conference presentations.

An issue raised at the 1988 and 1989 Women and Theatre Program preconferences of ATHE is the threat of assimilation of feminist work. From a materialist perspective, it is important for feminists to ask "who profits" from feminist theory and criticism. Is it publishers, who find they can sell books with "feminist" or "woman" in the title? Is it male critics and practitioners who have begun using some of the vocabulary of "gender" analysis in articles and productions, perhaps to "sell" plays and productions that may not be feminist at all? Will feminism be worked into the curriculum and then slowly changed and watered down by oversimplification? Will a few token women be given visibility and tenure, and large numbers of women, perhaps women of color, lesbians, or those with a working-class perspective, be pushed aside with the argument that if they were "good enough" they also would be visible and tenured? As feminist theory and criticism grow, it is important to raise such questions and keep them in mind.

For me, Dolan and Case raise a number of the most useful overall ideas for beginning to formulate feminist theatrical and dramatic criticism. The first is that feminists can regard theater as a laboratory. In a paper originally presented in 1984, Dolan questioned the age-old statement that the stage is a mirror of "real life" and asserted that from a feminist's perspective, "the theatrical mirror is really an empty frame." By questioning the entire apparatus of theater's representation of women, feminists can "deconstruct gender categories. If we stop considering the stage as a mirror of reality, we can use it as a laboratory in which to reconstruct new, non-genderized identities. And in the process, we can change the nature of theatre itself."[49] A year later Case wrote: "The feminist in theatre can create the laboratory in which the single most effective mode of repression—gender—can be exposed, dismantled and removed."

Case continues on to the second idea, that divisions in feminist politics offer strategic opportunities. She advocates using both radical and materialist theories as "tactics to be employed when they were useful in either dismantling the patriarchal structure or aiding in the cultural revolution." In a conservative environment, a radical approach might provide "a new theory and an alternative practice," while in an environment that was already radical, a materialist approach would bring up issues of race and class. She says this would not be "playful pluralism," but rather "a guerrilla action designed to provoke and focus the feminist critique."[50]

By searching out insights gained by feminists in literary criticism, anthropology, psychology, and film theory, the feminist dramatic critic can develop a broader perspective. By keeping in mind the possibilities presented by the political divisions of feminism and the stages of feminist criticism, as well as the contributions of black and lesbian feminist theorists, that broadened perspective can be deepened. And by using that perspective as a tool for developing "tactics" in criticism and practice as well as for the "laboratory" that theater can become, feminists can indeed transform dramatic criticism.

CHAPTER 2

Feminist Literary Criticism: The "Resisting Reader"

Feminist Literary Criticism Surveyed

Literary criticism has historically been applied to drama, and there is now a growing body of feminist literary criticism of plays. Some of this is first-stage "image of women" criticism, which points out patterns in writing by men in which, for example, the female characters suffer or die in order for the male characters to grow or continue on their life journeys. Other, second-stage criticism focuses on patterns in women's writing such as repressed fears and anger expressed through coded plot lines and character types. Third-stage theory-centered work tends to focus on language itself and the connections or lack thereof between words and "reality." The entire field deserves close scrutiny for its application to drama.

Feminist literary criticism has a long and complicated history; fortunately, several review essays and histories help to summarize its activities. First among these are five review essays in literary criticism that appeared in *Signs: Journal of Women in Culture and Society* between 1975 and 1989.[1] The first two authors, Elaine Showalter and Annette Kolodny, have become major figures in the field. Kolodny summarized her essay and that of Showalter, saying that both "reveal a kind of critical stasis." She went on to describe feminist literary criticism (in 1976) as "appearing in various

21

guises, unevenly practiced, more like a set of interchangeable strategies than any coherent school or shared goal orientation. . . ."[2] By 1979 Sydney Janet Kaplan listed some needs of the field: widening of the canon to include third-world and working-class women and works written before the nineteenth century, and "more informed considerations of aesthetics based on feminist principles."[3] Cheri Register in 1980 had her own complaints: not enough work on changing the canon or on female aesthetics and too much ahistorical analysis in books such as *The Madwoman in the Attic,* with its use of Harold Bloom's idea of "anxiety of influence," which asserts that "a literary work embodies the author's struggle against the intrusion of 'his' predecessors into his own imagination." Adopting Bloom's analysis means that "since literary precedent is almost the only determining factor considered, literature becomes its own context, leading to a claustrophobic involution."[4]

Five years earlier Register had formulated three subdivisions of feminist criticism: "image of women," "criticism of female authors," and "prescriptive." About the latter she said that "it may become the crux of feminist criticism in the future. It is a 'prescriptive' criticism that attempts to set standards for literature that is 'good' from a feminist viewpoint." She went on to say that this type of criticism is defined "in terms of the ways in which literature can serve the cause of liberation." It must perform one or more of five functions: "(1) serve as a forum for women; (2) help to achieve cultural androgyny; (3) provide role-models; (4) promote sisterhood; and (5) augment consciousness-raising."[5] After that essay came out, many feminist critics wrote in passionate detail that feminist criticism must not be prescriptive. Their tone nearly equalled Register's in its absoluteness. Though her specific suggestions have not, for the most part, been pursued, she did raise the issue of the need for a political dimension to feminist criticism, linking it to its roots in the women's movement.

Two other essays are more recent overviews of the field. Elaine Showalter, in trying to write a history of feminist criticism for a special issue of *Tulsa Studies in Women's Literature* titled "Feminist Issues in Literary Scholarship," talked about "women's time" and feminist history and described her own personal history in the field. She outlines the main trends of thought very well:

> Since 1975, feminist criticism has taken two theoretical directions, that of the Anglo-American focus on the specificity of

women's writing I have called *gynocritics,* and that of the French exploration of the textual consequences and representations of sexual difference that Alice Jardine has named *gynesis.* . . . Gynocritics is, roughly speaking, historical in orientation; it looks at women's writing as it has actually occurred and tries to define its specific characteristics of language, genre, and literary influence, within a cultural network that includes variables of race, class, and nationality.

Gynesis . . . seeks instead to understand the space granted to the feminine in the symbolic contract. . . . repossess as a field of inquiry all the space of the Other, the gaps, silences, and absences of discourse and representation. . . . very little attention is paid to women writers.[6]

Sydney Janet Kaplan supplies a useful overview of the theories of feminist criticism, including those of Showalter, in her essay "Varieties of Feminist Criticism."[7] After surveying many of the books and anthologies published in the 1970s and early 1980s, she summarizes the work of several critics of that same period, devoting the most space to Elaine Showalter's strengths and weaknesses. Kaplan ends by pointing up the marked difference between Showalter's theory of literature as part of a "female subculture" and Annette Kolodny's call for a multiplicity of theories, or "playful pluralism."

The difference between these two main theorists comes up in many overviews, including those of Toril Moi and Janet Todd.[8] Moi divides her book into sections on "Anglo-American" (actually only American) feminist criticism and French feminist theory. Each part is a brief introduction to the principal theorists, together with Moi's reservations about each, reflecting her materialist feminist point of view. Once again, Showalter and Kolodny get full treatment. She does, however, favor the French over the American theorists. Janet Todd points this out in her book, published three years later, and proceeds to defend the more historical approach of the American theorists over the French. Todd is also a materialist and adds the British materialist feminist theorists Cora Kaplan and Michelle Barrett, as well as "men in feminist criticism," to her discussion.

In the most recent review essay in *Signs,* Betsy Draine addresses herself to the American/French split, which she summarizes and likens to the biblical story of two mothers arguing over one baby. Today, however, some critics are not relying on the "wisdom of Solomon" to give one school of thought custody of the field, but are addressing themselves to both sides of this debate. The critics and theorists she most applauds are those who acknowledge differences and express "a determination to deal with theoretical conflicts by addressing the opposition directly." She calls these books "attempts to achieve clarity through dialogue."[9]

While the overviews so far mentioned have represented one woman's voice summarizing what she has seen and read, there are many anthologies of critical essays that present a multiplicity of voices. Taken together, they form another type of summary. In the 1970s, five such anthologies spoke about what feminist criticism was and could be.[10]

Images of Women in Fiction actually dealt with first- and second-stage criticism, from Joanna Russ's observations on the plot options available to a woman writer in "What Can a Heroine Do? or Why Women Can't Write" to Josephine Donovan's analysis of the sentence structure of several women novelists in "Feminist Style Criticism." *Feminist Literary Criticism* included Cheri Register's previously mentioned essay advocating prescriptive criticism, other essays beginning to explore the idea of a feminist aesthetic, a "dialogue" between a text- and a context-oriented feminist critic written by Carolyn Heilbrun and Catharine Stimpson, and a summary piece by editor Josephine Donovan, which pointed to common threads and future trends in feminist criticism. *The Authority of Experience* contained thirteen essays on specific works or writers of fiction and three of a more theoretical nature that tried to define feminist criticism. *Feminist Criticism* included reprinted articles from MLA meetings in 1971 as well as Annette Kolodny's "Some Notes on Defining a 'Feminist Literary Criticism,'" which had originally been published in 1975. *Women Writing and Writing About Women* moved toward third-stage criticism, with Mary Jacobus's "The Difference of View," which touched on French psychoanalytic theory, and Laura Mulvey's "Feminism, Film and the Avant-garde," which brought film theory and semiotics into the discussion, along with Elaine Showalter's "Towards a Feminist Poetics."

In the late 1970s, Showalter and Kolodny each wrote two essays that put forth their theories.[11] As mentioned earlier, Showalter called for a "gynocritics," which would center on women's writing and not adapt male modes of criticism. Kolodny stressed "playful pluralism," which would allow a free interplay of ideas from many sources (including male modes). Each has had supporters and detractors. Both were influential, particularly in the 1970s, but the issues have become more diverse in the 1980s. While Showalter has moved into the somewhat broader area of "gender" criticism, which tends to include study of both male and female gender constructs, Kolodny has recently issued a warning about the academic minefields of the 1980s being in some ways more dangerous than those of the 1970s because men have entered the field and begun to take it over.[12]

Five anthologies of essays on feminist literary criticism and theory and one reader with very short selections, all six published in the 1980s, make a large cross-section of work from the last fifteen years available to a wide audience.[13] Elizabeth Abel and Elaine Showalter each edited anthologies that include a good selection of essays from the 1970s up to about 1982. Showalter's includes an excellent bibliography up to 1984. The Gayle Greene and Coppélia Kahn book contains more recent work and stresses cultural and other contexts rather than individual literary texts. Nancy Miller edited papers given at a conference in 1984 that show the beginnings of movement toward integration of French theories with Anglo-American ideas. The reader edited by Mary Eagleton contains by far the largest number of contributions (over sixty), but they are not dated and many are only one or two pages long. Many hard-to-locate British sources are included, and Eagleton has written brief introductions to the five subdivisions of excerpts. Showalter's most recent anthology, as previously mentioned, addresses the issue of "gender" rather than feminism and includes contributions by male as well as female critics.

Other books of the 1980s show some specific trends in both literary criticism and feminist thought. One such direction is that of "narrative strategies,"[14] which is also a topic addressed in film theory. Another trend is called "critical studies" or "cultural criticism,"[15] in which several fields (such as history, science, literature, and film) are studied in an interdisciplinary manner by means of feminist theory.

Two other topics of thought in literary studies, canon formation and deconstruction, have been used by both feminists and nonfeminists in recent years. A particularly heated exchange about the canon took place in 1983–84 in *Critical Inquiry*.[16] The great difficulty of changing attitudes toward what conventionally has been studied has begun to be overcome by feminist criticism and activism, and more works by women are now more commonly included in anthologies and courses. Deconstruction is advocated by Gayatri Chakravorty Spivak in a number of essays[17] and has its other supporters as well who are trying to adapt this man-made tool to feminist uses.[18] In theater, frequently a text is deconstructed through production. These topics—narrativity, critical studies, canon formation, and deconstruction—as well as others might easily be adapted by feminist dramatic critics. However, it is necessary to look at a single theorist to see most clearly the usefulness of literary theory for analysis of drama.

Judith Fetterley and the "Resisting Reader"

Finding a single, representative theorist/critic in feminist literary criticism to apply to drama was much more difficult than in the other three fields. Literary criticism frequently incorporates insights from other fields, and so finding a uniquely "literary" theory is not easy to begin with. My criteria for selection of the theory, as mentioned earlier, included how influential the theorist has been and how fruitful her ideas are when applied to drama. There was no single essay with the impact of those of Rubin in anthropology or Mulvey in film. In considering "literary" theories, I was drawn toward those that focused on the reader of the text, with the obvious thought that the reader of a novel in many ways resembles the reader of a play and the audience at a play performance.

Beginning in the 1970s a number of literary critics' work was grouped together under the title of "reader-response" criticism.[19] One of the first to combine the ideas of the reader and feminism was Judith Fetterley, whose 1978 book *The Resisting Reader: A Feminist Approach to American Fiction* analyzed four short stories and four novels written by American men in the nineteenth and twentieth centuries.[20] Both the basic concept of the feminist reader as a "resisting reader" and some of Fetterley's specific insights into American fiction are applicable to American drama as well. Several feminist theater critics have already alluded to her "resisting reader" concept in the introductions of their books.[21] I would like to look at her ideas in more detail.

Fetterley begins her introduction with several blunt statements: "Literature is political" (xi). "American literature is male" (xii). "America is female; to be American is male; and the quintessential American experience is betrayal by woman" (xiii). She then elaborates on these ideas briefly, using the works of fiction she will analyze at length later in the book.

The middle section of her introduction articulates the basic concepts of her approach, drawing first from work by Elaine Showalter and Lee Edwards:

> Though one of the most persistent of literary stereotypes is the castrating bitch, the cultural reality is not the emasculation of men by women but the *immasculation* of women by men. As readers and teachers and scholars, women are taught to think as men, to identify with a male point of view, and to accept as normal and legitimate a male system of values, one of whose central principles is misogyny. (xx)

She goes on to define terms and provide what she considers necessary measures to deal with this condition:

> Clearly, then, the first act of the feminist critic must be to become a resisting rather than an assenting reader and, by this refusal to assent, to begin the process of exorcizing the male mind that has been implanted in us. . . . While women obviously cannot rewrite literary works so that they become ours by virtue of reflecting our reality, we can accurately name the reality they do reflect and so change literary criticism from a closed conversation to an active dialogue. (xxii–xxiii)

The remainder of the introduction explains the choices and ordering of works in the rest of the book, explaining that "these eight are meant to stand for a much larger body of literature" (xxiv). Some of the specific insights she draws from these eight works are especially applicable to plays as well.

Fetterley finds Washington Irving's "Rip Van Winkle" a paradigm of making male a potentially "universal" desire: the avoidance of responsibility is defined as escape from Dame Van Winkle. Rip is a prototypical American character, a "nice guy" like Huck Finn, who escapes civilization, which is drawn as a nagging woman, by sleeping for many years. He also achieves "access to life in an all-male world, a world without women, the ideal American territory" (6), in which he observes the reverse of what happens in his village, or "men who invade female territory and dominate it and drive the women out" (7). Then Fetterley asks the important question: "But what is a woman to do with 'Rip Van Winkle'?" She cannot identify with Rip, "for the fantasy he embodies is thoroughly male and is defined precisely by its opposition to woman," but she cannot identify with Dame Van Winkle either, because

> Dame is not a person: she is a scapegoat, the enemy, the OTHER. Without name or identity other than that of Rip's Dame, she is summarized, explained, and dismissed through the convention of stereotypes as a "termagant wife," a shrew, a virago. . . . Dame Van Winkle is a male mechanism, not a woman. (9–10)

At this point, Fetterley comes close to what is going on now in third-stage feminist theory, talking about the falsity of the entire representation of "Woman." But she goes on to explain very clearly the mechanism whereby, while not identifying with either Rip or Dame, a female reader is manipulated by the text into "taking Rip's side and laying all the blame on Dame Van Winkle; that is the way the story is written" (11). The result is that the female reader moves against herself, scorning the inscription of "Woman" that Irving has provided and in doing so acting "just like a woman," that is, confirming the view of "women as each other's natural and instinctive enemies" (10). This same mechanism is at work in many plays as well as novels and needs to be exposed by the "resisting reader" feminist critic as one of the most pernicious effects of "negative images" of women.

Many of Fetterley's other specific observations are useful as well. In four of the eight works, female lovers or wives die, two at the hands of their mates, but in all cases the death is used to draw sympathy for the male character. In Nathaniel Hawthorne's "The Birthmark," a scientist experiments on his wife in order to remove a birthmark from her face, and in the course of doing so he kills her. The husband has many high-minded rationales for "perfecting" his wife, but in point of fact Hawthorne "obscures the issue of sexual politics behind a haze of 'universals' and clothes the murder of wife by husband in the language of idealism" (xv). The story points out that "the motive underlying the desire to perfect is the need to eliminate" and "the idealization of women has its source in a profound hostility toward women" (24). As Fetterley says, the story is about "how men gain power over women . . . without ever having to relinquish their image as 'nice guys'" (33). In the course of the story the wife comes to

share her husband's revulsion at the birthmark by internalizing his attitudes, and, as Fetterley points out, her "situation is a fictional version of
the experience that women undergo when they read a story like 'Rip Van
Winkle'" (32). She eventually wishes to die rather than to continue to
remind him that he has failed to remove her "mark"; she gets her wish.

Fetterley necessarily took a more naive approach to reading than some
theorists today who, for instance, have the use of recent film theory. But
the drama critic can easily go back to her work and apply it to the American dramatic canon. By using the strategy of resisting, feminist critics can
point out ways the text inscribes masculinity, help change the process of
reading for women, and suggest ways that performances of a text can resist
its own immasculation of the audience. The process of intervention in
production can be very effective in increasing audience awareness of what
it is watching, hearing, and feeling. As Fetterley points out, fiction texts
cannot be rewritten; they can only be read by women who then "name
the reality they do reflect." In the case of drama the process by which
feminists "name the reality" in a written text can have a material effect
on the performance text. "In making available to women this power of
naming reality, feminist criticism is revolutionary" (xxiii).

The most obvious candidate for application of Fetterley's ideas is the
grandfather architect of serious American drama: Eugene O'Neill. O'Neill
was very familiar with the nineteenth-century theatrical tradition, but
pushed on to found a tradition for the twentieth. He is the only world-
recognized American playwright from the period before World War II
and was a winner of the Nobel Prize for Literature in 1936. His long
writing career spanned the 1910s to the 1940s. His plays used a variety
of styles and influences, from Greek tragedy to Expressionism, from Ibsen
to Strindberg. One play that lends itself very well to examination by a
feminist "resisting reader" was written during his last period of productive
work and was the first of his two or three "masterpieces": *The Iceman
Cometh*.

Eugene O'Neill's *The Iceman Cometh*

I realize in retrospect that I have been a resisting reader of O'Neill since
my high school days. As I read his plays, I felt distanced, on the outside
looking in. I was taught he was the greatest American playwright, but I

could not find my way into the plays. I read criticism. O'Neill was supposed to have great emotional depth; where was it? As an undergraduate, I tried further. I saw productions, read more critics. Where was this greatness?

On my own I sought out the women involved in the Provincetown Players, the group that first produced O'Neill. I found myself drawn much more to the plays of Susan Glaspell than to those of O'Neill. I discovered, reading between the lines of her history, that the negative reactions of a few prestigious critics to her Pulitzer Prize for a play in 1931 had sent her back to writing novels, never to try the stage again. I tried to sell her to *Ms.* magazine as a "Lost Woman." She was too obscure for them in 1975. Disappointment at every turn. I am particularly pleased that Glaspell is now receiving increased attention, in large part because of feminist critics.[22]

I finally found myself responding in some emotional, as well as intellectual, way to the Broadway production of *A Moon for the Misbegotten* and the film of *Long Day's Journey into Night*. Colleen Dewhurst had finally gotten through to me, and then Katharine Hepburn. But I could not scale the mountain. *The Iceman Cometh* was certainly big enough. It was waiting to be climbed, but I kept slipping back. A decade after undergraduate school I read Judith Fetterley and others, and it became clearer. I was resisting what that play and many of O'Neill's other plays said. I did not believe his "women" were women and I did not like what he made them say. It turns out I had been acting in self-defense.

The Iceman Cometh was written by O'Neill in 1939 and published in 1940, but not produced until after World War II, in 1946. It was not very well received in its first production, but took its current place as one of O'Neill's most important plays after its revival, directed by Jose Quintero and starring Jason Robards, in 1956. The play portrays the denizens of a seedy Greenwich Village bar in 1912 over a period of two days. The total cast consists of sixteen men and three women. Of the male characters, two are police who enter briefly at the end, two are major characters who come to the bar on the days portrayed, three are the owner and bartenders of the bar, and the other nine are regular customers. Most of the characters also live in rooms over the bar. The three women are described by O'Neill as "street walkers."[23] The play, in four acts, is roughly twice as long as a conventional play and is usually performed with a dinner break in the middle.

The plot of the play revolves around the visit of Hickey, a salesman whose arrival at Harry Hope's saloon for Harry's birthday is eagerly awaited by its regulars because he can be counted upon to buy them all drinks and give them a laugh. This visit turns out to be different. Hickey seems to have reformed. He has as his mission to get all his friends to give up their respective "pipe dreams" and actually do the things they have been talking about doing for years. Parallel to Hickey's story is that of new arrival Don Parritt. Don's mother, Rosa Parritt, is a famous anarchist who has been recently betrayed to the police and is in jail. Parritt comes to the bar for advice from ex-anarchist Larry Slade, who may be his father. Over the course of the play the regulars listen to Hickey, go out into the world and find their pipe dreams cannot be made to come true, and return depressed. By the end of the play, Hickey reveals, in various stages through an enormous monologue, that he has killed his wife, Evelyn. Parritt reveals that it was he who betrayed his mother to the police. Police come and arrest Hickey (who has called them himself), and Parritt, having gained Larry's tacit permission to do so, throws himself out the window of his room above the bar.

This brief description does not begin to give an account of all of the characters and subplots. The male characters provide a microcosm of the "world" for many critics: there is a failed policeman, a failed lawyer, a failed journalist, two failed political activists, two failed military men who continue to fight their personal version of the Boer War, and a token Negro. The length of the play and the repetitions within it convey the impression of being in a bar with a number of rambling alcoholic dreamers. By the end they restore balance for themselves by accepting Hickey's final self-deception, that he is insane.

Critics have pointed out that the overall theme is that of the necessity of pipe dreams for man's [sic] survival. The play has been analyzed from a vast number of perspectives, some of which point out analogies to Christ, the disciples, and the last supper; some to a few Russian plays of the underclass, such as The Lower Depths; and some to the plays of Strindberg and Ibsen, particularly to the theme of Ibsen's The Wild Duck. The sheer size, the microcosm of characters, and the number of literary, social, religious, and philosophical references of the play have helped make it the subject of a large body of critical discussion. It is clearly an "important work" for most critics, second only to Long Day's Journey into Night in the O'Neill dramatic canon. Ironically, it is almost never produced because of the large number of middle-aged male actors required to perform it. Good middle-aged actors are rare and expensive, a fact that merits a materialist analysis.

From a feminist perspective, the play itself presents several problems. The women characters shown on stage are three stereotypical whores, while the three wives and one mother who are constructed offstage through the men's dialogue are scapegoats, blamed for most of the men's problems. Women have no lives of their own in this play. To paraphrase a joke that is connected to the play's title, the iceman cometh, but the women are not even breathing hard.

The women who appear on stage are of the profession that would realistically put them into this milieu; they perform a necessary function and are therefore allowed into this otherwise all-male world. From the beginning of the first act, the topics of whores, pimps, and betrayal are linked. When one character asks Rocky, the bartender, "Vere is your leedle slave girls?" (11), Rocky immediately counters with:

> Hell, yuh'd tink I wuz a pimp or somethin'. Everybody knows me knows I ain't. A pimp don't hold no job. I'm a bartender. Dem tarts, Margie and Poil, dey're just a side line to pick up some extra dough. Strictly business, like dey was fighters and I was deir manager, see? . . . What if I do take deir dough? Dey'd on'y trow it away. (12)

Parritt, early on, says, "I never want to see a whore again! I mean, they always get you in dutch" (37). The reason for this outburst is clarified near the end of the play: "about selling out, it was the tart the detective agency got after me who put it in my mind" (247). His early statement sets an attitude of mistrust toward the three "tarts" we do see. When Margie and Pearl enter ("*Rocky:* Aw, dat's on'y my two pigs" [61]), they are described by O'Neill as, among other things, "sentimental, feather-brained, giggly, lazy, good-natured and reasonably contented with life" (62). They are undifferentiated whores with hearts of gold, in other words. They describe their customers from the evening as "all-night guys" who "didn't bother us much dat way," but kept the girls awake all night talking to each other (64). The girls' time on stage during the play is spent in the same way: the men do not bother them for sex, but only want to talk among themselves. Their pipe dream is that they are "tarts," not whores, though at the very end of the play they come back drunk from a night at Coney Island and Margie says, "Gangway for two good whores!" (255). They are quickly set straight by Rocky: "Yuh're tarts, and what de hell of it?" (256).

Cora is older and more aggressive, and has a larger role in the play than the other "tarts." Her pipe dream of marrying the other bartender, Chuck, comes to the same end as the other pipe dreams. She has something of a relationship to Hickey, probably because he used her services at some point, and her reactions to Hickey give her a few moments of importance in the play. She sees Hickey before he comes to the bar and begins to prepare the regulars by saying Hickey is "different" and "funny" (75). She also participates in his long, final monologue by cutting in at several points, inserting her own point of view (the only such moments in the play). When Hickey describes joking with the whores he used while on the road, Cora empathizes: "Jees, all de lousy jokes I've had to listen to and pretend was funny!" (236). When he describes getting a venereal disease from one of them, Cora adds, "Yeah. And she picked it up from some guy. It's all in de game" (237). Finally, she responds before anyone else to the conclusion that Hickey killed his wife: "Jees, Hickey! Jees!" (239). But these moments of assertion come during the dramatic climax of the play, which clearly belongs to Hickey.

The need for a feminist resisting reader approach is even more acute in terms of the female characters not seen on the stage. Among them are two "bad wives." Marjorie Cameron is the wife Jimmy "Tomorrow" Cameron blames for his drinking. As Hickey says in act 2:

> We've all heard that story about how you came back to Cape Town and found her in the hay with a staff officer. We know you like to believe that was what started you on the booze and ruined your life.... I'll bet you were really damned relieved when she gave you such a good excuse. (141)

Jimmy's case seems at this point to be analogous to Hickey's running story of how Evelyn cheats on him with the iceman. But in the end Hickey admits that Evelyn is not guilty of this sin. Marjorie may well be guilty, but her guilt, her very existence, is something that the characters, like the audience, take on faith based only on Jimmy's words.

Harry Hope's wife Bessie, often referred to as "poor old Bessie," is responsible for Harry's inability to leave the bar since her death twenty years earlier. He claims he simply cannot go on without her sainted presence. But from the beginning this construction of Bessie is questioned, in a whisper, by Larry: "By all accounts, Bessie nagged the hell out of him" (50). Harry continues to maintain the goodness of Bessie, until after he ventures out of the bar at Hickey's prompting and is disillusioned with the world he finds. It then slips out from Harry that Hickey is "a worse gabber than that nagging bitch, Bessie, was" (202). Bessie and Evelyn are linked when Hickey says Evelyn was shot through the head and Harry responds, "To hell with her and that nagging old hag, Bessie" (204). The only good wives are dead wives, and it is dying that makes them good.

Rosa Parritt, patterned to some degree on Emma Goldman, is presented by Don as a "bad mother" because she was too busy with the anarchist movement to pay attention to him (26). Her bigger sin, however, was that she was too interested in her own freedom, including having sex with whomever she wished. Parritt suffers guilt for turning his mother in to the police and blames her for causing this guilt. He feels that what he has done to her is to cause her living death because she loved freedom so much. The analogy between Parritt and Hickey is announced over and over, in the dialogue and in the parallels in their cases. The ultimate similarity between them is the way in which the "truth" about how each felt about the woman he "killed" is revealed, step by step, in the course of the play.

In act 1, Rosa is constructed as a "bad mother" but an activist who was sold out to the police by somebody. Evelyn is known to the regulars as a character in Hickey's running joke about finding her in bed with the iceman. In act 2, Parritt tells Larry he felt that living with his mother was "like living in a whorehouse" (125), that "I know damned well you've guessed—," and that he sold out the movement because of patriotism. "But I never thought Mother would be caught" (128). At the end of the act, Hickey says, "I'm sorry to tell you my dearly beloved wife is dead.... she's at peace. She's rid of me at last.... all that Evelyn ever wanted out of life was to make me happy" (150–51).

The next levels of "truth" are revealed in act 3. Now Parritt admits it was not because of patriotism that he sold out his mother, but, rather, "It was just for money! I got stuck on a whore and wanted dough to blow in on her and have a good time!" (160). Hickey gives more clues: "It was a bullet through the head that killed Evelyn," to which Larry responds,

"You drove your poor wife to suicide?" Hickey then sets them straight: "No, I'm sorry to have to tell you my poor wife was killed" (204–5). At this point the perception is, as Harry says, "Somebody croaked your Evelyn, eh? Bejees, my bets are on the iceman!" (206).

The main feature of act 4 is Hickey's monologue. He says he thought of killing himself, but that would have broken Evelyn's heart, so "there was only one possible way. I had to kill her" (227). Harry assumes he did it because of the iceman. Hickey counters that he joked with her about her taking a lover, just as he told the iceman jokes at the bar. Even after he gave her venereal disease, Evelyn insisted on forgiving him, causing guilt. "I even caught myself hating her for making me hate myself so much. . . . You have to begin blaming someone else, too" (239). Finally, Hickey's confession leads Parritt to admit about Rosa, "I didn't give a damn about the money. It was because I hated her." Hickey relives the moment after the murder, when he said to Evelyn, "'Well you know what you can do with your pipe-dream now, you damned bitch!'" (241). Both men admit they acted out of hate, but both quickly move to justify that admission. Hickey concludes, "I must have been insane" (242), and Harry picks up on that as a way to excuse the turmoil of the past two days. After Hickey is taken away by police, Parritt falls back on blaming "the tart the detective agency got after me" and elicits permission from Larry to kill himself. Both men leave the stage, having told their whole "truth."

The closure of the play comes from the revelation to the audience of what the men "really" felt about these women. In resolving this mystery, the men reveal much about themselves and their hatred of women, but the women still remain mysteries, at least for women in the audience who may try to reconstruct them. The pieces given are tainted, and there are too many missing. But in the drama of watching the men reveal their "truths," the only role Woman can play is that of scapegoat.

Fetterley's observations about "Rip Van Winkle" are very relevant to this play's world of men sleeping and drinking to avoid responsibility in the "real" world. The unseen women represent responsibility, whether they are nagging shrews or "too good" women who induce guilt. As Fetterley says, "But what is a woman to do with" *The Iceman Cometh?* She cannot identify with the men, because they constantly construct themselves in opposition to women; she cannot identify with the thin stereotypes of whores on stage or the shrews, boring wives, and "bad mother" offstage. She can, however, be drawn into blaming the offstage women for the men's problems, if she is not "resisting" enough. She needs not to make that move against herself, especially during Hickey's long, seductive monologue. It is constructed to make her do just that, to immasculate the reader and audience, to make everyone "feel" for Hickey while blaming, or at least ignoring the interests of, Evelyn. Hickey remains a complex, difficult, but "nice" guy to the end. Like Willy Loman's, his downfall is constructed as the tragic "death of a salesman," and his wife is an absence.

Analogies to "The Birthmark" are equally clear. Like that story, the play cloaks the murder of wife by husband through use of "universals" and "ideals," such as the religious symbolism and the "pipe dream" theme. The play is actually an elaborate justification for murder in which the emotions of the murderer are placed center stage and the life of the victim is totally obscured. The betrayal of a mother by a son is similarly cloaked in talk of "the movement" and later Freudian overtones of sexual jealousy. The implication is that Rosa's independent sexuality is responsible for her own imprisonment, Larry's drunken condition, and Parritt's suicide. If she had only been an asexual, proper mother figure, none of this would have happened.

A feminist reading of *The Iceman Cometh* can lead toward feminist intervention in its production. Such intervention might go in one or more of several major directions. One direction could be that of foregrounding gender by performing the play with an all-female cast, or with a cross-gender cast, with men playing the women's roles. The women could play the roles as if they were men, or as if they were actresses trying the play on for size (and perhaps rejecting it). Another approach could try to represent the missing women by having actresses in a different part of the stage area "act out" those roles, particularly those of Rosa and Evelyn. Without adding a word of dialogue, the actresses would be constant presences, nonverbally making themselves more "real" than the script itself allows. A third choice would be to foreground the fact that the offstage women are not "real," but rather male constructs. This could be done in a number of ways, including the use of film images, slides, masks, and puppets to represent the missing women. Their absence in this case would be noticed, but no attempt would be made to say that the "women" indicated in the script reflect actual women's lives by having actual women play them. The constantly shifting "facts" and "truths" about the women could be indicated, showing the contradictions in the men's testimony and the lack of ability to "know" the women. This last approach in particular would have the effect of deconstructing the script and indicating the contradictions within it. A woman reader of this play could find an "effeminized" production just the tool needed to resist immasculation by it.

One observation I have made in thinking through the American canon using Fetterley's ideas is that they seem to apply more easily to plays written by males who identify themselves as heterosexual than to works by those who identify themselves as homosexual or bisexual. The percentage of the latter among American playwrights in the canon is higher than among American male fiction writers in the canon. A larger number of plays than novels seem not to immasculate the female reader in the precise way Fetterley articulates. After having made my choices, I realized that the male-written plays analyzed in this book are all written by heterosexual-identified playwrights (O'Neill, Miller, Shepard), perhaps because those by homosexual-identified playwrights (such as Wilder, Williams, Inge, and Albee) bring up much more complex issues of gender. The influence of sexual preference on the writings of female and male playwrights is certainly an issue worthy of future feminist dramatic criticism. A feminist response to *A Streetcar Named Desire* or *Who's Afraid of Virginia Woolf?* requires more complex theories than literary criticism alone may be able to provide. To formulate this type of response, and many others, the feminist critic needs to examine other fields of feminist theory.

CHAPTER 3

Feminist Anthropology: The "Exchange of Women"

Anthropology, Liminality, Theater, and Women

Anthropology, through pointing out variations in cultures throughout the world, foregrounds the fact that cultures are constructed. It questions assumptions that may appear "natural" or "invisible" from within a given culture. In the realm of sex-gender arrangements, it can show that definitions of "masculine," "feminine," "men's work," "women's work," and many other concepts are culturally relative constructs. Feminist theorizing within anthropology points out male biases in the field itself and fills in gaps in fieldwork. It places a new emphasis on women's roles in kinship, labor, and governing structures.

Aspects of anthropology have been used for quite a while as tools for theatrical performance as well as critical analysis. For example, the late Victor Turner wrote extensively about the relationship of ritual and theater. One of the concepts he discussed is liminality, "literally 'being-on-a-threshold,' [which] means a state or process which is betwixt-and-between the normal, day-to-day cultural and social states and processes . . . a time of enchantment when anything *might*, even should, happen."[1] It is a stage in any rite of passage between one state and the next, a free zone between, say, childhood and adulthood. It is a place that can be inhabited by women who are resisting cultural categories and a position that needs to be examined as a perspective from which feminist theorizing and criticizing can take place.

But all anthropological theories, as well as their applications, need to be examined for their biases about women. Turner's description of the women in a theater workshop in which students developed some of his fieldwork into performance is revealing. After hearing Turner's wife describe girls' puberty rituals in the tribe under consideration, the women "began a rehearsal with a ballet, in which women created a kind of frame with their bodies . . . in which the subsequent male political action could take place." But, according to Turner, this "feminist mode of staging ethnography" just "didn't work." After pausing to ask, but not begin to answer, the question "Does a male ethnographer, like myself, really understand or take into full analytical account the nature of matrilineal structure . . . ?" he goes on to state that since the piece was about a struggle for political office, which was a "male affair," the women's framing of the scene "diverted attention from the fact that these particular dramas were essentially male political struggles."[2]

This brief example shows that in anthropology, as in any field, a theorist may advance ideas that can be useful for feminist work, but the theorist may simultaneously demonstrate biases that must be questioned. Stopping to ask the question of potential bias is not enough. Describing women's actions is not enough. In order for a feminist perspective to emerge, women themselves must be heard, must put their bodies and their words on the stage and on the page. And feminist critics can then join with other critics in pointing out what does and does not "work," and for whom.

To help with the task of rescuing anthropological concepts for feminist dramatic criticism, it is useful to look at how women within anthropology have gone about analyzing and changing perspectives in their field.

Feminist Anthropology Surveyed

The earliest stages of feminist anthropology can be traced through several anthologies of articles published between 1974 and 1981. In general, researchers in the field did first- and second-stage work simultaneously, criticizing male bias in previous anthropological theorizing and reporting and inserting the experience of women into the work where it had not previously appeared. By the 1980s, what I would call third-stage work had begun, questioning basic assumptions of the field, investigating the entire question of gender construction, and moving toward heavier use of symbolic anthropology and linguistics. From the beginning there has been strong Marxist input from some practitioners and a generally higher level of socialist/materialist awareness than in many other fields.

The first feminist anthology was *Women, Culture, and Society*, edited by Michelle Z. Rosaldo and Louise Lamphere. Its sixteen essays do four things, according to their editors: "suggest that sexual asymmetry [females and males treated differently] is not a necessary condition of human societies but a cultural product accessible to change," that asymmetry "means different things in different places," that variations from culture to culture "can be accounted for by particular social and economic factors," especially women's contributions to subsistence, and that they "present a challenge to future thinking in anthropology."[3] The first three essays are the most theoretical, with Rosaldo, Nancy Chodorow, and Sherry B. Ortner all presenting aspects of the idea that biology is not necessarily destiny for women, but that culture constructs women's roles. This theme is dominant through much of feminist anthropology, from these early essays up to the present.

The second anthology, *Toward an Anthropology of Women*, edited by Rayna R. Reiter, came out one year later. The collection had many similarities with the first, aiming to "subject our notions of male dominance to specific analysis, and push us to understand that it is anything but natural."[4] It contains several essays with a Marxist perspective, including the most widely influential of all: Gayle Rubin's "The Traffic in Women: Notes on the 'Political Economy' of Sex."

The movement toward a linguistic approach to anthropology could be seen five years later in the essays in *Women and Language in Literature and Society*, edited by Sally McConnell-Ginet, Ruth Borker, and Nelly Furman.[5] The three editors represented three areas of study: linguistics, anthropology, and literary criticism. Each contributed an essay on her specialty; Borker's was a survey of research on language and anthropology through the late 1970s. In 1981 an anthology devoted to symbolic anthropology was published: *Sexual Meanings: The Cultural Construction of Gender and Sexuality*, edited by Sherry B. Ortner and Harriet Whitehead. In their introduction the editors point out that in most cultures "the differences between men and women are in fact conceptualized in terms of sets of metaphorically associated binary oppositions" and proceed to describe several: "nature/culture," "self-interest/social good," and "domestic domain/public domain," in each of which female is associated with the former and male with the latter.[6] Symbolic anthropology uses semiotic methods similar to those used in film theory.

In a 1982 review essay in *Signs,* Jane Monnig Atkinson summarizes some of the topics and trends in feminist social and cultural anthropology from 1979 to 1982. She points out that feminist anthropologists have begun to question each other's assumptions and that some find that "dichotomies such as domestic/public and nature/culture, and premises such as universal sexual asymmetry, are ideological constructs that have their history in Western European society," making them less broadly useful than originally asserted. At the same time, these concepts, especially universal sexual asymmetry, continue to have supporters who counterargue the attacks.[7]

Atkinson outlines four traits of recent work: (1) the assertion that "sex roles and gender concepts must be seen as products of history and society, not as reflections of inherent human sexual natures," a longstanding idea going back to Margaret Mead; (2) a "strong commitment to historical analysis, which Marxist analysts have been calling for for some time"; (3) "the non-Marxist camp has displayed a strong commitment to comparative study," such as much of the work in the Ortner and Whitehead anthology; and (4) "the growing concern among anthropologists with the interplay of situation, context, and meaning," which is being seen in new ethnographic studies whose fieldwork and writing reflect a feminist theory from their inceptions (245–47). She ultimately calls for what I would consider a third-stage approach, "not simply to supplement our knowledge but indeed to realign our disciplinary approaches" (255).

In a *Signs* essay five years later, Marilyn Strathern describes the "awkward relationship" between the fields of feminism and anthropology. She sees interdisciplinary feminism as perpendicular rather than parallel to anthropology and other fields, and therefore sees a difficulty in shifting paradigms (patterns or models) from feminism to anthropology. She focuses on "some of the problems that disciplinary practices can put in the way of responsiveness to feminist theorizing" and specifically "the investigator's relationship with his or her subject."[8]

A recent survey of the field, *Feminism and Anthropology,* by Henrietta

L. Moore,[9] reflects a clear materialist approach and can serve as a useful introduction to many of the current issues surrounding the relationship of feminism to any traditional field of study, including theater. The body of the book deals with social anthropology in relationship to sexual asymmetry, construction of gender, sexual division of labor, capitalism, and women's relationships to the state. In her first chapter Moore defines feminist anthropology as "the study of gender, of the interrelations between women and men, and of the role of gender in structuring human societies, their histories, ideologies, economic systems and political structures" (6). She outlines three phases of the field: (1) the "anthropology of women" phase, in which male bias within the field was criticized; (2) the move toward the "study of gender" rather than "study of women," and the work of defining the category of "woman" itself; and (3) the current phase, in which emphasis is on acknowledging the differences among women, "the building of theoretical constructs which deal with difference," and "looking at how racial difference is constructed through gender, how racism divides gender identity and experience, and how class is shaped by gender and race" (11). The issues brought up by this last phase are the most current ones in many fields of feminist work, including theater.

Gayle Rubin and the "Exchange of Women"

One essay that appears again and again in virtually any discussion of feminist anthropology and often in application to many other fields is Gayle Rubin's "The Traffic in Women" (1975).[10] For instance, in the October 1985 "Staging Gender" issue of *Theatre Journal,* Rubin was quoted in three out of six articles.[11] Several things may account for the article's popularity. In it she gives brief, accessible explanations of some of the theories of Karl Marx, Claude Lévi-Strauss, and Sigmund Freud (as interpreted by the French analyst Jacques Lacan, whose interpretation often is used by feminists in psychology and film theory). Written while the author was still a graduate student, the essay conspicuously avoids the dense jargon that often mars such writing. Clear explanations are rare even today, let alone in 1975 when many women beginning feminist research were in great need of them. Rubin relates the theories to each other and criticizes each for its weakness vis-à-vis women, such as the failure of both

Freud and Lévi-Strauss to notice anything wrong with the treatment of women as objects in the systems they are describing. Because of the number of disciplines included in Rubin's work, there is indeed "something for everyone" here, and hers is a model of interdisciplinary possibilities. Politically, she brings up materialist issues that the average liberal or radical feminist would not think about, though for some materialists she is not sufficiently socialist.

Since the article itself is mostly a summary of a number of complex theories, its main points can only be superficially summarized. Rubin states at the beginning that in reading the works of Lévi-Strauss and Freud "one begins to have a sense of a systematic social apparatus which takes up females as raw materials and fashions domesticated women as products," though neither Lévi-Strauss nor Freud "turns a critical glance upon the processes he describes" (158). She feels that in feminist hands each man's theories can provide tools with which to describe oppression of women and others in the "sex-gender system" of a society. The Marxian description falls short of doing this because, according to Marx, "human beings are workers, peasants, or capitalists; that they are also men and women is not seen as very significant" (160). In fewer than four pages three sacred bulls are, if not killed, severely wounded. Rubin does, however, pick up on Engels's methodology in *The Origin of the Family, Private Property, and the State,* because he deals with sexuality as an issue. Though she disagrees with his results, she adapts some of his method, namely the examination of kinship systems.

In discussing the anthropological view of the kinship system, Rubin mainly uses Lévi-Strauss's *The Elementary Structures of Kinship,* which further developed the idea first advanced by Marcel Mauss of the giving and receiving of "gifts" as an organizing principle of a society. Lévi-Strauss added the ideas that "marriages are a most basic form of gift exchange, in which it is women who are the most precious of gifts" and that "the incest taboo should best be understood as a mechanism to insure that such exchanges take place between families and between groups" (173). Rubin goes on to set forth the essence of her contribution:

> If it is women who are being transacted, then it is the men who give and take them who are linked, the woman being a conduit of a relationship rather than a partner to it....

To enter into a gift exchange as a partner, one must have something to give. If women are for men to dispose of, they are in no position to give themselves away. . . .

The "exchange of women" is a seductive and powerful concept. It is attractive in that it places the oppression of women within social systems, rather than in biology. Moreover, it suggests that we look for the ultimate locus of women's oppression within the traffic in women, rather than within the traffic in merchandise. (174–75)

The difference between Rubin and Lévi-Strauss is that she takes the time to say that the exchange of women is not "natural," nor a cultural necessity. Neither is the phallic privilege of most psychoanalysis. Lacan discusses Lévi-Strauss in a 1968 essay and, according to Rubin, "suggests that psychoanalysis is the study of the traces left in the psyches of individuals as a result of their conscription into systems of kinship" (188). Rubin gives a brief account of Lacan's reinterpretation of Freud, which is a good starting point for much work in psychology and film, as well as anthropology:

The phallus is a set of meanings conferred upon the penis. The differentiation between phallus and penis in contemporary French psychoanalytic terminology emphasizes the idea that the penis could not and does not play the role attributed to it in the classical terminology of the castration complex. . . .

. . . Castration is not having the (symbolic) phallus. Castration is not a real "lack," but a meaning conferred upon the genitals of a woman. . . . The presence or absence of the phallus carries the differences between two sexual statuses, "man" and "woman." (189–91)

In a section titled "Oedipus Revisited" Rubin describes the Freudian oedipal phase, as seen by Lacan, and the differences between the boy's and the girl's experience of it. The boy "gives up" his mother in exchange for which "the father affirms the phallus in his son." In this way the boy "exchanges his mother for the phallus, the symbolic token which can later be exchanged for a woman" (193). The girl, however, "has no 'phallus,' she has no 'right' to love her mother or another woman, since she is herself destined to some man." The girl turns from the mother to the father, but "the father does not give her the phallus in the same way that he gives it to the boy." When she realizes that she has a "lack," she takes her place in society. "She can 'get' the phallus—in intercourse, or as a child—but only as a gift from a man. She never gets to give it away" (193–95).

The rest of the article points out the good "fit" between the Freudian and Lévi-Strauss systems and proceeds to develop the beginnings of a "political economy of sex" in the manner of Marx and Engels.

Nancy Hartsock, in her book on feminist historical materialism, admits Rubin's popularity and influence, but objects to the abstract rather than materialist base of her argument. Hartsock questions "the extent to which feminists can borrow from phallocratic ideologies without their own analyses suffering in consequence" and calls for a "specifically feminist epistemology."[12] In essence, she prefers the sexual division of labor to the more symbolic "exchange" as a basis for analysis. But many other theorists have taken Rubin as a starting point for their own theories.

Male Homosocial Desire

In the field of feminist literary criticism, for example, Eve Kosofsky Sedgwick has used Rubin's "exchange of women" paradigm in her book *Between Men: English Literature and Male Homosocial Desire*.[13] In an earlier article on the same subject, Sedgwick defines "male homosocial desire" as "the whole spectrum of bonds between men, including friendship, mentorship, rivalry, institutional subordination, homosexual genitality, and economic exchange,"[14] and illustrates how the "traffic in women" takes place in consonance with these bonds in two examples from English literature: William Wycherley's play *The Country Wife* and Laurence Sterne's novel *A Sentimental Journey*.

Sedgwick makes several points about *The Country Wife* that will later be useful in analyzing *Death of a Salesman*:

"To cuckold" is by definition a sexual act, performed on a man, by another man. Its central position means that the play emphasizes heterosexual love chiefly as a strategy of homosocial desire. . . . I will discuss it [*The Country Wife*] as an analysis of several different paths by which men may attempt to arrive at satisfying relationships with other men.

. . . The status of the women in this transaction is determiningly a problem in the play: . . . their ambiguous status of being at the same time objects of symbolic exchange and also, at least potentially, users of symbols and subjects in themselves. The play teaches that women are in important senses property, but property of a labile [unstable] and dangerous sort.[15]

Sedgwick's book deals mainly with eighteenth- and nineteenth-century novels written by men, but her use of Rubin, combined with the idea of "erotic triangles" taken from René Girard, does have some application to contemporary American drama. The core of her approach is that "patriarchal heterosexuality can best be discussed in terms of one or another form of the traffic in women: it is the use of women as exchangeable, perhaps symbolic, property for the primary purpose of cementing the bonds of men with men."[16] About erotic triangles she notes Girard's observation that "the bond that links the two rivals is as intense and potent as the bond that links either of the rivals to the beloved," and that most of the triangles he discusses are "those in which two males are rivals for a female."[17] Today, of course, it is possible to trace many other kinds of triangles as well.

Arthur Miller's *Death of a Salesman*

If O'Neill's later work is the granddaddy, Arthur Miller's *Death of a Salesman* is the daddy of contemporary American drama. It has achieved both critical and popular success and a continuous record of production since its Broadway opening in 1949. Its basic family structure, that of father, mother, and two dissimilar sons, is a classic one. From the first family in the Bible to O'Neill's *Long Day's Journey into Night* (written before, but produced after *Salesman*), this family structure has been a popular one for "serious" male writers in all genres. For a feminist critic looking at images of women in drama, one problem with this family structure is the complete absence of the daughter role. The only female role portrayed within the family is that of wife/mother.

In the case of *Salesman,* the other female roles are also problematic. Of a cast of thirteen characters, five are female. Other than wife/mother Linda Loman, the other four are barely characterized, except in some form of sexual relation to one of the male characters. Miss Forsythe and Letta are "girls" picked up by Happy and his brother in a restaurant. Jenny is the secretary of Willy's friend, Charley; her main function is to be impatient with Willy and to be the object of some sexual byplay on Willy's part.

> *Willy:* Jenny, Jenny, good to see you. How're ya? Workin'? Or
> still honest?
> *Jenny:* Fine. How've you been feeling?
> *Willy:* Not much any more, Jenny. Ha, Ha![18]

The other female is the unnamed character in the flashback scenes in Willy's mind. Known only as "The Woman," she is the receptionist with whom Willy has an affair in a Boston hotel room; the discovery of this affair by Willy's son is the climax of the play and the beginning of the downfall of both father and son. Though there is some indication that each of these women works outside the home for money, they all are traded, in Rubin's terms, as objects in some variety of exchange among the men in the play and do not in any way function as independent subjects.

The main action of the play involves the triangle of Willy and his two sons, Biff and Happy. The wife and mother, Linda, is restricted before the play begins by her characterization in the very first stage directions. She is described as loving and admiring of her husband, who overtly demonstrates his longings, "which she shares but lacks the temperament to utter and follow to their end" (12). That is the end of the possibility of that woman acting on her own behalf. She was traded long ago and has no "temperament" to change the terms of the deal. Though at times a triangle may include Linda, for the most part Biff-Willy-Happy is the male homosocial connection that is dramatized and has the greatest importance attached to it. Both sons love the father and have competed for his love in different ways since childhood, never receiving enough of the right kind. Biff has a pattern of "stealing" and Happy one of "whoring" to try to compensate for the lack of satisfactory paternal relationship. One has turned to merchandise, the other to women as objects of exchange. Happy illustrates Sedgwick's point about the exchange of women facilitating bonds between men. He offers Biff women both to boast and to ingratiate himself, and at the same time he competes with his brother in using women. But that "winning" is not enough because he still loses to Biff when it comes to Willy.

Neither son has married, though at thirty-four and thirty-two they are at an age at which, were they women, they would be called "old maids." Both the sons reveal their attitudes toward women and marriage in the scene between them in their old bedroom early in act 1. Biff concedes: "Maybe I oughta get married. Maybe I oughta get stuck into something," while Happy lists among the objects his money can buy "my own apartment, a car, and plenty of women" (23). Women are clearly objects of exchange for Happy. Several times in the play he "gets" a girl for his brother or offers to do so in order to gain his brother's favor. Before the play begins they have been out on a double date, and the restaurant scene in act 2 shows Happy in the act of picking up one girl and arranging another for his brother. He does not get satisfaction, however, from his conquests. He admits to Biff that "it gets like bowling or something. I just keep knockin' them over and it doesn't mean anything" (25). His main reason for conquest is competition with the other men at his office, an extension of his competition with Biff. The girl he was out with before the play begins was engaged to a man "in line for the vice-presidency of the store" where he works, and "maybe I just have an overdeveloped sense of competition or something, but I went and ruined her, and furthermore I can't get rid of her. And he's the third executive I've done that to." He even admits, "I don't want the girl, and, still, I take it and—I love it!" (25). What he loves is winning something that the men "better" than he is don't have—yet.

Happy competes using women in order to gain some relationship with the other man involved in each instance. In the case of the executives he even goes to their weddings. The reason he offers "any babe you want" to Biff is that he wants to gain Biff's approval. But Happy has always come out second in the race for his father, and he knows it. His whoring is an unconscious (perhaps) patterning after his father, and he can still do it because he was not scarred by having witnessed the climactic "primal scene" Biff walked in on in a Boston hotel room at the age of seventeen.

That scene has put Biff off women almost entirely, except for the gestures he makes to accept the "gifts" of women he receives from his brother. Biff tries to gain his father's approval through setting up a business deal. Happy has already "succeeded" at work; when he feels needy or guilty he says he will get married. At the end of act 1, after Willy has encouraged Biff in his business endeavor, Happy says out of nowhere, "I'm gonna get married, Mom. I wanted to tell you" (68). And after Biff and Willy have their last exhausting confrontation, ending with Willy's strong feeling that Biff loves him, Happy adds his contribution: I'm getting married, Pop, don't forget it. I'm changing everything. "I'm gonna run that department before the year is up" (133–34). He will bring home a woman for his parents in exchange for their approval of him.

The play moves toward that primal "climax" when Biff finds his father in a hotel room with "The Woman" (she has no name; she is mythic but also anonymous, like the sex Willy enjoys with her). The message of that scene, like that of the restaurant scene that immediately precedes it, is that women are what come between men and their fathers. "The Woman," Miss Forsythe, and Letta function in the play as whores, with no power and almost no characterization. They are objects who can be traded but, since they are not wives, are not totally under the men's control. They can "tempt" a son to desert his father in a restaurant or, worse, cause a father to alienate his son. Women are indeed property of a dangerous sort.

The overpowering impression the play leaves is that, for men, sex with women is empty, mothers and wives are necessary but ineffectual, and the most important thing is to bond successfully with other men. The problem is that this play has become a paradigm for what the "serious American play" should be. It is among the half-dozen most lauded plays in the canon, and among the most imitated. Most playwright "sons" of Arthur Miller try to beat the old man at his own game sooner or later. Even Sam Shepard's "family" plays can trace some of their roots to this play. It is the *Oedipus Rex* of American drama for many people, and the continuation of its centrality effectively cuts women's experience out of consideration for "serious" drama. Some of the old patterns must be changed to allow for woman-as-subject, not traded object, to be seen on the stage.

Feminist criticism can begin to point out and criticize these dominant patterns. Awareness can lead to innovations in production that undercut the unthinking acceptance of canonical scripts. A feminist director might cast the sons in *Salesman* with female actors, to point up the absence of daughters in the play. A completely cross-gender cast would show a three-woman triangle given prominence, pointing up the absence of such triangles in plays and the lack of mother-daughter engagement of any kind in the American dramatic canon. A racially mixed cross-gender cast would also disrupt expectations about whose "American dream" is being presented in the play. In a different vein, the object-of-exchange quality of all the women could be underlined by having the female roles performed in a distinctively different style, such as that of oriental drama, using heavy makeup or masks, while the males performed in realistic style.

Awareness of the damaging images and lack of active female subjects in plays in the canon may also lead to the writing of plays in which women's roles are not so restricted. Toward this goal, we can look to the precedent of a few postwar plays written by women, particularly those plays that may not have been as readily accepted in the canon as were others in the same period.

Lillian Hellman's *Another Part of the Forest*

Produced in the same period as *Death of a Salesman,* Hellman's *Another Part of the Forest* (1946) reveals a different view of the traffic in women: the female "property" is allowed to act and speak for herself as a subject, even as we see her being exchanged by the men on stage as if she were an object. Hellman also includes a black woman servant, whose presence in the play underscores the particular intersection of race, gender, and property in the America of 1880.

Produced seven years after *The Little Foxes, Forest* portrays some of the same characters as its better-known sister (which was the source for a popular movie starring Bette Davis), but at an earlier point in their lives. It was, in effect, a "prequel." In *Foxes,* set in 1900, Regina has married Horace Giddens, has a daughter, and is scheming to gain some economic control of her life, which has always been circumscribed by her brother, Ben. Her other brother, Oscar, is overbearing toward his wife, Birdie.

Back in the 1880 setting of *Forest,* Regina is a girl of twenty in love with Birdie's cousin, John. In the course of the play the family balance of power shifts from Regina's father, Marcus, to her brother, Ben, when Ben receives damaging evidence from his mother, Lavinia, against Marcus. Ben thus gains the upper hand in his siblings' love lives, and it is foreshadowed

51

that Regina will be forced to marry Horace, and Oscar, who loses his "working-girl" love, Laurette, will be forced to marry Birdie, whose family is in desperate financial straits.

Like *Salesman, Forest* is a family play, with a mother, father, and two dissimilar sons, but in this case the usually missing daughter is present. Unlike *Salesman* this is a "history play," set in an earlier period than when it was written, but it deals with the roots of the same post–World War II materialism that Miller used in his play. Both are basically passing-along-of-the-phallus plays, but, unlike Miller, Hellman chooses to keep the father alive at the end of the play, pushed to the side but still a physical reminder of the passage of power. Perhaps sons, more than daughters, actually need to "kill off" the father to achieve their climax.

Hellman includes in the play two black servants, Coralee and Jacob, as well as a number of examples of the racism of the time and place she portrays. These characters may seem problematic from a contemporary feminist perspective, but are believable figures within the conventions of a realistic play of the period. Both are seen performing serving functions, such as bringing food into a room or announcing guests. Jacob is sent on errands, but Coralee is given a larger role in the play; she is the constant companion of Lavinia, whom everyone considers to be crazy. Coralee and Lavinia together form much of one side of the ethical argument in the play. And by virtue of her race, Coralee is a visible reminder that there are factors other than gender that influence a woman's ability to arrange, or not arrange, for her own exchange.

In this play, as in *Salesman,* there are five female characters in a cast of thirteen. By using the idea of the exchange of women to examine the images of the women, we can see that all five have enough characterization and perform significant enough actions to be seen as active agents, even though by the end of the play three have left or are leaving town and the other two are to be married off at Ben's discretion. We see them struggle within their circumscribed roles, even though they are overpowered in the end.

Hellman shows the rise of a son and the passing of a father from power, but underlines the fact that is is due to social and accidental factors, not the inevitable superiority of sons over daughters. Regina is just as worthy a successor to her father as Ben, but due to the fact that Regina decided to sleep late one morning and Ben was around when Lavinia decided to share her secret, Ben received the tool with which to overpower the old man. The way they are portrayed in this play allows women to be participants, though not winners, in the game.

Lavinia embodies several aspects of stereotypical female behavior, but at the same time tells truths and determines the outcome of the play. She has the power of information, but lacks the ability to use it for her own sake. Hers is the last presence in each of the first two acts, leaving a lasting impression in audience minds. Her leave-taking, with Coralee, is the next-to-last moment of the play. But she appears to be both passive and crazy. There are many reasons suggested for Lavinia's madness in the play, her husband's brutality being one of them. Her passivity, which has been called the "deception of passivity" by one critic,[19] may also be seen as a response to her husband, with a well-suppressed anger under it. In act 3 she tells Ben that she has always been afraid of Marcus, and of Ben, too. "I spent a life afraid. And you know that's funny, Benjamin, because way down deep I'm a woman wasn't made to be afraid."[20] For one moment we see the strong young woman she once must have been and the painful self-awareness she has of her subjugation. Gayle Rubin offers some insight into Lavinia: "The creation of 'femininity' in women in the course of socialization is an act of psychic brutality," and it "leaves in women an immense resentment of the suppression to which they were subjected" but also "few means for realizing and expressing their residual anger."[21] There is room in the play for production elements, such as Lavinia's use of a mask or her omnipresence on the stage, that would stress Lavinia as a source of female power that is being suppressed.

Coralee, who is forty-five to Lavinia's fifty-nine years of age, is given complete charge of the "lady" of the house, who is at times as dependent as a child. At the same time, Coralee demonstrates the fact that race is a factor that even further restricts women's ability to trade themselves or control their lives. She is seen trying to prevent trouble for Lavinia and herself by encouraging Lavinia to avoid irritating her husband, but in the same scene she stubbornly withholds from Marcus information the audience knows she has. Her exit from that scene is not indicated, and it is interesting to speculate on a production in which the two servants, or the pair of Coralee and Lavinia, might be a pervasive presence in the play. Coralee and Lavinia share the last moments of the first act, in which Lavinia repeats her dream of teaching black children back in her old hometown as expiation for her sin.

> *Lavinia:* Such sin I couldn't even tell you.
> *Coralee:* You told me.

Coralee sees the problems involved in Lavinia's plan ("Maybe they'd be scared of a white teacher coming among them"), but in the end humors her charge. When Lavinia becomes depressed, Coralee suggests what has become a pattern for Lavinia: "I tell you what. Come on in the kitchen and rest yourself with us" (351–52). In act 2 Coralee defends Lavinia as best she can ("You all have been teasing her, and she's tired"), and at the end of the play she accompanies Lavinia on that woman's suddenly realized dream of returning to her hometown.

But Coralee is present in Lavinia's words at other points in the play, including the long story near the end in which Lavinia narrates the events of the night during the Civil War in which she and Coralee saw Marcus betray the South and cause the death of many local soldiers: "Coralee caught cold. I had to nurse her for days afterward. . . ." (384). Later Ben uses Coralee's presence as a witness to help pressure his father. Lavinia tells Marcus to apologize to her and to Coralee and to give some money to Coralee's family. This instance of a white woman speaking for her black servant is at once a further delineation of Lavinia's character and an absence from the stage of the speaking black woman subject. Again, the possibilities for countering this absence in production are intriguing. But whenever Coralee is present and speaking she presents a rare representation of any black female within the dominant canon.

Regina, Birdie, and Laurette are all twenty years old: a peak age for being exchanged. The irony is that Laurette, who is looked down upon as socially inferior to every other white person in the play, is the only woman who is in a position to trade herself, and does so. In agreeing to marry Oscar, she goes to the highest bidder, but she herself controls the transaction. When Oscar cannot come up with the price she is asking, she leaves for New Orleans without him, in search of more prosperous bidders.

Regina and Birdie have Ben trading them, cementing the social and economic bonds among three families as he does so. Birdie tries to do some trading herself, when she asks for a loan on property that is not hers to trade. In the end Ben gives her the loan for his own reasons, but it is made clear that the only commodity that will successfully be traded will be Birdie herself, in marriage to Oscar, arranged by Ben.

Regina tries to resist her mother's fate of powerlessness within a loveless marriage by trying to arrange for her own marriage to John Bagtry. She uses sex to lure him, but in the end lacks the economic power to carry out her plans and is forced to align herself with Ben. In this way we see that Ben will have the power to trade her to the Giddens family in return for their money and prestige, which, along with Birdie's cotton, will make him even more powerful than his father had been. By the end of the play it is clear that neither Ben nor Regina will allow love to stand in the way of a quest for power. The action of *The Little Foxes,* held in the back of the mind while reading or seeing this play, shows the economic prosperity combined with lovelessness that become Ben and Regina's fate. But *Forest* gives an understandable picture of how both got that way, and of how Regina's options were limited by her gender.

Salesman presents a powerful male view of female characters as objects. It has influenced subsequent American drama as well as the definition of "serious" drama. *Forest,* written during the same period, presents women as objects struggling to be subjects, not better objects. *Forest* makes explicit connections between the exchange of women and the economic benefits that accrue to men. Besides cementing his bonds to other men, Ben's control over all the women in the play guarantees that he will be the economic "winner," which in turn cements his control of the men as well. *Salesman* minimizes the economic factors involved in the exchange of women and stresses the homosocial bonding it guarantees.

In all levels of criticism, from the 1940s to the present, Hellman's play has been considered "minor" and Miller's "great." But by paying attention to all aspects of women in the plays, and by looking at plays in terms of the exchange of women and of male homosocial desire, a new perspective is obtained. The evaluations of "minor" and "great" might be reversed from this new perspective, or the question might be asked, great for whom? A feminist analysis might lead to very different styles of production for these realistic plays, or might affect the decision to produce or not to produce them in the first place. But there are more issues to pursue for feminist criticism. While anthropology stresses social relations among individuals, psychology stresses the individual herself and the process by which that individual's identity is formed.

CHAPTER 4

Feminist Psychology: Mother-Daughter Bonding

Feminist Psychology Surveyed

Psychology, by offering various interpretations of identity formation and function, provides tools for the analysis of character in drama. It also provides insights into relationships among characters and, at points, intersects with anthropology and sociology. It tends to look for "universal" patterns of development that apply across many cultures, but too often examines only white Western subjects to do so. Feminists in psychology point out the absence of women in theorizing by men and give importance to the construction of female identity, the role of language in gender construction, and relationships among women. The mother-daughter bond has received considerable emphasis, in an effort to compensate for the fact that it was virtually ignored earlier. A major criticism by materialist feminists of the use of psychology, and particularly of psychoanalysis (based on Freud), is that attempts to find some universal "essence" of, say, femaleness, do not take historical and material differences into consideration and are therefore essentialist. However, some aspects of psychology are useful for feminist criticism and therefore well worth investigating.

Feminist psychology has created a much larger, harder-to-summarize literature than the feminist literature of the other social sciences, but several overview essays introduce the issues addressed. In a review essay in *Signs* in 1979, Mary Brown Parlee described four basic areas of research in the psychology of women: (1) critiques of traditional psychological research on women; (2) empirical research from a feminist perspective; (3) theoretical contributions to psychology arising from feminist research; and (4) theoretical contributions to problem-centered research (of an interdisciplinary nature, such as research on rape).[1] In an article published six years later, Parlee discusses what she calls three "promising problems" currently being addressed by the psychology of women: (1) power, sex, nonverbal communication, and conversational interaction; (2) connectedness versus separation from others; and (3) psychology of female reproductive processes. Under the second "problem" she mentions Nancy Chodorow's "very important book," which "describes the way social arrangements whereby females are the primary caregivers for both girls and boys come to produce fundamental psychological differences between women and men."[2]

The introduction to a book of essays on feminist psychoanalytic literary criticism summarizes some of the specific topics taken up by critics working at the intersection of psychology and feminism: the relationship of feminism and Freud, feminist interest in Freud's case of Dora, object-relations theory and Nancy Chodorow's work, the influence on French feminists of Jacques Lacan's rereading of Freud, and the relationship of feminism and deconstruction. The writers acknowledge the usefulness of Chodorow's work but say it lacks "the particular consideration of the relation between gender as she describes it and representation" and add that the subject of representation is taken up by French feminists.[3]

The ideas of French feminists are among the most interesting in the field of psychoanalysis. Yet their work is particularly dense and difficult to describe, in part because they embody their ideas, such as connections between women and nonlinear thinking, in their writing itself, and in part because of the problems inherent in translating from French into English. Several American writers and journals have attempted to translate the language and ideas of the "new French feminisms" into Anglo-American terms.

One of the most concise of these "translations" appears as the abstract of an article by Ann Rosalind Jones. First comes context:

French theories of femininity, using Derridian deconstruction and Lacanian psychoanalysis, centre on language as a means through which men have shored up their claim to a unified identity and relegated women to the negative pole of binary oppositions that justify masculine supremacy.[4]

Next comes the work of the four most prominent French feminist writers:

Julia Kristeva posits the concept of the semiotic, a rhythmic free play she relates to mother-infant communication, and looks for in modernist writers. Luce Irigaray emphasizes *différence,* a totality of women's characteristics defined positively against masculine norms, and imagines a specifically feminine language, a *parler femme.* Hélène Cixous celebrates women's sexual capacities, including motherhood, and calls for an *écriture féminine* through which women will bring their bodily energies and previously unimagined unconscious into view. Finally, Monique Wittig rejects this emphasis on *différence,* arguing that women must be understood not in contrast to man but in historical terms as subjected to oppression. (80)

Jones points out that Irigaray, for instance, in a book published in 1974, "suppressed verbs, posed questions rather than writing assertions, used telegraphic and exclamatory phrases," used puns, and later added "double or multiple voices, broken syntax, repetitive or cumulative rather than linear structure, open endings" (87–88) in order to embody a feminist writing style. French feminists' work rarely falls into any one conventional genre, often combining them, "feminizing" them, or forming new categories. "Fiction" and "nonfiction," "art," and "criticism" are labels not readily applicable. But Jones does outline four main methods used in "Franco-feminist criticism since the 1970s": deconstruction, attention to silences, "decoding of feminine/semiotic modes of writing and close reading of the politics of style" (96).

Both liberal and materialist feminists tend to find these writers' emphasis on the uniqueness of women's bodies as essentialist or to find a basic contradiction between any kind of rational discourse, such as criticism, and the nonrational philosophies expressed. Jones summarizes some of the objections to this work:

59

> Is there any point in applying feminist versions of more recent
> critical methods to such texts? What is to be gained from psycho-
> analysing a text whose express purpose is to reveal its writer's
> unconscious, from aiming the X-ray techniques of structuralism
> at a text written to overthrow the "ready-made grids" of binary
> opposition, or from turning the historicist ideology-critique of
> Marxism upon futuristic texts written *against* ideology? Franco-
> feminist criticism resists any easy pluralist assimilation. (93)

There are probably more differences than similarities among these
four women. Irigaray and Cixous are both clearly expressing radical feminist values. Kristeva most often writes criticism of male writers who do (in
her term) "semiotic" writing. Wittig is a materialist and the furthest from
psychoanalysis of the four. Yet from the moment of their appearance in
English, they have been grouped together. The years 1980 and 1981 saw
an outpouring of articles on the "new French feminisms," beginning with
a book of that title that presented a number of pieces in one place in
English for the first time. This was followed by four journals, two feminist
and two not, with entire issues devoted to either French feminism or
"difference."[5] Many of the primary texts by the "big four" have been
translated and published,[6] and a number of books and articles are devoted
to explaining and differing with the French.[7]

Their influence on feminist theater criticism can begin to be seen in
the pages of the "Staging Gender" issue of *Theatre Journal* (October
1985). Three essays use French theories and one analyzes Cixous's play
Portrait de Dora, which has been successfully produced in France and
England and published in French and (twice) in English.[8] *Dora* combines
in a highly theatrical manner many of Cixous's theoretical ideas with a
text "about" one of Freud's most-discussed cases. The play's importance
to feminist dramatic criticism can be gauged by the fact that *Dora* is
discussed by, among others, both Case and Dolan in their books, two
other critics in Enoch Brater's *Feminine Focus,* and one critic in the 1989
"Women in the Theatre" issue of Modern Drama.[9] In that same journal
issue, some of the work of Irigaray and Kristeva is used by feminist critic
Elin Diamond to begin to develop a theory of feminist mimesis.[10] By the
late 1980s the French theorists were beginning to be seen much more as
the distinct individuals they are, while discussion of their ideas in-

tensified.[11] On the other hand, there are many other branches of feminist psychology.

The liberal feminist approach to the field is expressed by the essays in a recent volume that answer no to the questions asked in its chapter headings (other essays answer yes): "Are Women More Likely to Be Mentally Ill?" "Are Menstruating Women at the Mercy of Raging Hormones?" "Do Women Fear Success?" "Can Sex Differences in Math Achievement Be Explained by Biology?" "Should Mothers Stay Home with Their Young Children?"[12] One of several radical feminist approaches to psychology is developed in a best-selling book by a Jungian analyst that relates archetypes of goddesses to psychoanalysis.[13] A materialist perspective is shown in the attention paid in the literature of the field—in a special issue of the journal *Women & Therapy*,[14] for instance—to the issues of race and class as well as gender.

Much of North American feminist psychological theory is in the field of object-relations. Judith Kegan Gardiner describes the field as follows:

> Object-relations theory explains how the child becomes a person. It stresses the construction of the self in social relationships rather than through instinctual drives. In this terminology, "objects" include everything that the self perceives as not itself. That is, the maternal object is not the mother but the child's mental representation of its mother.[15]

Several names are repeatedly mentioned in articles, especially those related to feminist literary criticism. The three that occur most regularly during the 1970s in work on the area of mothering are Adrienne Rich, Dorothy Dinnerstein, and Nancy Chodorow. Between 1976 and 1978, each published a book that has become a classic in the field.[16] Coppélia Kahn summarizes what the three have in common:

> To begin with, they all regard gender less as a biological fact than as a social product, an institution learned through and perpetuated by culture. . . . Second, they describe the father-absent, mother-involved nuclear family as creating the gender identities that perpetuate patriarchy and the denigration of women. . . . Third (and most important), because a woman is the first

significant other through whom both girls and boys realize sub-jectivity, women in general become charged with the ambivalence of fear and desire which is the inevitable by-product of that pro-cess.[17]

Judith Kegan Gardiner does a good job of summarizing the ideas of these three theorists in her overview essay:

> According to Dorothy Dinnerstein (1976), the fact of female mothering means that both boys and girls learn to associate women as a class with infancy's powerful irrational needs and fears. . . .
> Nancy Chodorow explains the cycle whereby women wish to be mothers and succeed at their role. . . . As symbiotic mothers, they will perpetuate the cycle by distancing their sons while inti-mately merging with their daughters. As a result, the "masculine sense of self" is separate; the "feminine sense of self remains connected to others in the world" (Chodorow 1978, p. 169). . . . Adrienne Rich celebrates the power of mother love and sees all women as originally and potentially lesbian because all women first love another woman. She also describes lesbian rela-tionships as invested with the intensity and ambivalence of the mother-daughter bond.[18]

Gardiner points out that there are theorists who take a more negative view of this close mother-daughter bonding, stressing the fact that the daughter must struggle to separate out from the mother. Among these theorists are Jane Flax and Jessica Benjamin. In an essay published the same year as Chodrow's book, Flax discusses the nature of the struggle for individuation in a patriarchial society.[19] Benjamin, in a more recent essay, discusses what she sees as the weaknesses in some mother-daughter theo-ries and suggests going beyond these theories to stress, among other things, the father-daughter bond. She argues that "women lack a desire of their own." She goes beyond the theories that stress the father as agent for separating from the mother to the idea of both women and men as subjects (intersubjectivity) rather than object and subject:

Woman's desire, I believe, can be found not through the current emphasis on *freedom from:* as autonomy or separation from a powerful other, guaranteed by identification with an opposing power. Rather, we are seeking a relationship to desire in the *freedom to:* freedom to be both with and distinct from the other. This relationship can be grasped in terms of intersubjective reality, where subject meets subject.[20]

On the specific topic of mothers and daughters, Marianne Hirsch in 1981 named three main trends in research: (1) object-relations psychology, (2) Jungian studies, and (3) French feminist theory. She pointed out that "at the source of each of these important and useful feminist theoretical studies we find not only a male theorist but a developed androcentric system"[21]—a frequent criticism of nonradical feminist theories in many fields. She briefly surveys interview books and literary criticism on the subject, giving Nancy Friday's best-seller *My Mother / My Self: A Daughter's Search for Identity* much of the credit for the popularity of the subject of mothers and daughters, while criticizing its lack of scholarly rigor. In the end she cites the need "to invent new theoretical frameworks that allow us, in our study of relationships between women, truly to go beyond patriarchal myths and perceptions."[22]

Nancy Chodorow and the Mother-Daughter Bond

Nancy Chodorow wrote a number of articles before she published *The Reproduction of Mothering* in 1978. All of them are interdisciplinary in nature, but from 1971 to 1978 she moved from a sociological approach that was balanced between anthropology and psychology to a more psychological and finally an almost exclusively psychoanalytic approach. A 1971 mass-market anthology contains her early essay that tried to uncover the root of female oppression by exploring sex roles cross-culturally and developmentally. Chodorow relied heavily on Margaret Mead (anthropology), Karen Horney (psychology), and Simone de Beauvoir (philosophy) to develop her idea that female identity is devalued by society with the result that women must live through their children. She felt that as long as this model prevailed women would continue to "bring up sons whose

63

sexual identity depends on devaluing femininity ... and daughters who must accept this devalued position and resign themselves to producing more men who will perpetuate the system that devalues them."[23]

Chodorow's next essay appeared three years later in the first feminist anthropology anthology (mentioned in chap. 3). Several ideas entered her discussion at this point: the reproduction of sex roles and mothering, the centrality of the mother-daughter relationship, the use of a "largely psychoanalytic" perspective (though anthropology and sociology are still strongly present), and use of the writer's own experience in a "women's group that discusses mother-daughter relationships in particular and family relationships in general."[24] That footnote, prominently placed on the first page of the essay, made the statement that the researcher's own experience is to be used, not denied, in working in a feminist mode. Chodorow's methodology and evidence were later criticized, but her straightforward approach, checked against and contributed to by reality, may explain why her conclusions strike a chord of recognition in readers. In this piece she is describing both female and male patterns of development, concluding again that child care only by females creates specific sex roles in offspring. But she begins to pay more attention here to the close bonding between mother and daughter in the child's first few years (the preoedipal phase). While she stresses that the later oedipal crisis is resolved very differently by girls and boys and that the "girl cannot and does not completely reject her mother in favor of men, but continues her relationship of dependence upon and attachment to her,"[25] she continues to place the entire matter in a social context.

Chodorow's next essay,[26] even more explicitly psychoanalytic, was adapted for a section of *The Reproduction of Mothering*. Finally, the same year the book was published, she included much of its material in an article for *Feminist Studies*. She summarizes her work as follows:

> In a new interpretation of the feminine oedipus complex, I suggested that because women mother, the oedipus complex is as much a mother-daughter issue as it is one of father and daughter, and that it is as much concerned with the structure and composition of the feminine relational ego as it is with the genesis of sexual object choice. . . . and demonstrate that exclusive commitment to men, in spite of behavioral heterosexuality, is never completely established.[27]

She surveys some feminist psychologists' variations on the Freudian idea of penis envy—"She finds out her mother *prefers* people like her father (and brother), who have penises. She comes to want a penis, then, in order to win her mother's love"—and goes on to add that psychoanalysts assume heterosexuality, but "Rubin rightly reminds us that a mother's heterosexuality is not an inevitable given: it has also been constructed in her own development one generation previously."[28] Finally, she summarizes the girl's "turn to her father" during the oedipal phase:

> Every step of the way, a girl develops her relationship to her father while looking back at her mother—to see if her mother is envious, to make sure she is in fact separate, to see if she can in this way win her mother, to see if she is really independent.[29]

Much of *The Reproduction of Mothering* is devoted to the explication of various psychoanalytic theories of female development. Shakespearean critic Coppélia Kahn, in the previously mentioned essay on feminist psychological theories, advances the thought that "Chodorow reorients psychoanalytic theory with the feminist consciousness that has rejected the notion of woman as castrated man," and has found "in the mother-daughter relationship and in other relations among women, rich, various, and vital sources of feminine selfhood."[30]

Though her aim in this book is to account for the cross-cultural phenomena of predominately female child care and its role in the oppression of women, to my mind Chodorow's main contribution to feminist theory is to amplify earlier ideas and to focus attention on the previously neglected preoedipal period as critical in the development of the girl's personality and as functioning in a different way for female and male children. She translates many other people's theories into readable prose, making their ideas accessible to researchers in a wide range of fields. Like Rubin, she may be most important because of this translation as well as for maintaining a broader social perspective. Her book has been criticized for its methodology and evidence, for assuming heterosexuality rather than questioning it, for not including more analysis of race and class as well as gender, and for being essentialist,[31] but it continues to provoke discussion and to provide the very ideas with which to disagree.

Chodorow summarizes her description of the early bonding of mother and daughter in this way:

Because they are the same gender as their daughters and have been girls, mothers of daughters tend not to experience these infant daughters as separate from them in the same way as do mothers of infant sons. In both cases, a mother is likely to experience a sense of oneness and continuity with her infant. However, this sense is stronger, and lasts longer, vis-a-vis daughters. Primary identification and symbiosis with daughters is more likely to retain and emphasize narcissistic elements, that is, to be based on experiencing a daughter as an extension or double of a mother herself.[32]

When the girl reaches adolescence, she is struggling to separate out from her mother, but at the same time feels the close bonding. Mothers "desire both to keep their daughters close and to push them into adulthood," which makes the daughters anxious and "provokes attempts by these daughters to break away." This "leaves mother and daughter convinced that any separation between them will bring disaster to both"(135). The adolescent girl knows she is not really part of her mother, but may not feel the boundary between them. In separating, she may criticize her mother, or may "idealize the mother or the family of a friend"; she "may try in every way to be unlike her mother" and may "idealize a woman teacher, another adult woman or older girl, or characters in books and films, and contrast them to her mother"(137).

All this behavior may be familiar to women who have passed through adolescence, and particularly to mothers of adolescent girls, but it is all but missing from drama. In examining plays, it can be enormously useful to contemplate Chodorow's ideas that mothers experience a greater continuity with girl children than with boys and that daughters experience a sense of merging with their mothers that somehow persists into later life. They can also help in examining the differences between the representations of mothers by male and female writers. Stories of mothers and daughters told from women's points of view are extremely rare in drama. This absence needs to be examined along with the few plays that do exist. There are, of course, fewer female than male playwrights, but this fact alone does not account for the proportionately fewer plays about the mother-daughter relationship than about the father-son.

The absence may be accounted for more by the difficulties of the bond itself for the daughter, ambivalence about trying to break the bond, and the fact that the adult female playwright is probably still living with the results of the charged bond as she is trying to writing about it. While plays in which fathers and sons fight and are then in some way reconciled or separated by death serve to ease the oedipal tensions the son (playwright and audience member) may feel, the dramatizing of unresolved (and possibly unresolvable) preoedipal tensions between daughter and mother may be too painful, or too profoundly repressed, to be shown by the daughter. But a body of plays that do open up the subject may change the situation.

In the realm of solo performance, for example, Holly Hughes has written and performed a piece, *World Without End,* in which she "maps an intimacy redolent of incest, only the pair this time are mother and daughter: Holly and Mom."[33] The much more conventional, realistic play *'night, Mother* by Marsha Norman may be seen as a drama of the ultimate severing by the daughter of the bond with her mother, rather than a well-made play about suicide. As Jenny S. Spencer points out:

> The need for a daughter both to detach her love and yet to identify herself with the mother in order to acquire a "normal" gendered identity, *and* the need for a mother to support the child's project of autonomy despite mixed feelings regarding separation, is the drama that Jessie and Mama symbolically enact in the play.[34]

While the 1980s may allow for a lifting of repressions, it is interesting to consider a play, written during the Freud-conscious 1940s and 1950s, that glimpses rarely sighted depths in the mother-daughter bond.

Jane Bowles's *In the Summer House*

In the Summer House has not so far been accepted into the canon of American drama and so is unfamiliar to most people. Jane Bowles, born in New York in 1917, published her only novel, *Two Serious Ladies,* in 1943, the same year she began writing *In the Summer House.* She was encouraged by scene designer Oliver Smith, who periodically gave her money to write the play between 1943 and 1953 and eventually produced it on Broadway.[35] The play had a long gestation period.[36] It reached Broadway on 29 December 1953, starring Judith Anderson and Mildred

Dunnock, and was subsequently produced in New York City in 1964, 1977, and 1980.

The play is one of ellipses and absences, dreamlike and nonlinear at times, but with many of the trappings of realism. It concerns three pairs of mothers and daughters and is set in Southern California. Molly, eighteen, is the daughter of Gertrude; Vivian is their fifteen-year-old boarder, and Mrs. Constable is her mother; the third pair is a Mexican woman, Mrs. Lopez, and her daughter Frederica. The first and third scenes of act 1 are set in Gertrude's garden; the second is on a beach. Act 2's two scenes are set in a small restaurant called the Lobster Bowl. The time is "the present" and covers a period of fourteen months. Millicent Dillon, Bowles's biographer, describes the plot:

> In the course of the play Vivian drowns—either by falling from a cliff or being pushed from it by Molly. Gertrude marries Mr. Solares and prepares to go off to Mexico. But before she leaves Molly declares her love for her mother so violently that Gertrude is frightened. However, she goes to Mexico and Molly marries Lionel, a young man who works at a nearby restaurant, the Lobster Bowl. . . . He and Molly stay, in a chaste marriage, in a room above the Lobster Bowl. Mrs. Constable, with Vivian dead, has become an alcoholic and hangs around the restaurant to be close to Molly and Lionel.
>
> In the last act Gertrude, unhappy with her life in Mexico, returns to reclaim Molly from Lionel. In one version of this act Gertrude drags Molly away, after convincing her that she is violent and dangerous to others, and Lionel is left alone. In another version, Molly runs out and kills herself. In the published play Molly runs off with Lionel, and Gertrude is left alone. (228–29)

As Dillon points out, Bowles changed the ending several times. The published version still seems to end rather abruptly, but this lack of satisfying closure makes the play seem more modern today than many other examples of 1950s realism. "Like Jane's life, the play was based on a precarious balance, the absence of finality, even the evasion of ending. All of the endings, even the final one, seem forced." The critical reception in 1953 was mixed, in part because "the dilemma portrayed on the stage seemed to reviewers to be nothing but the trivial and neurotic arguments

68

of 'female crackpots'"(230). A feminist evaluation of the play finds much more there.

In terms of Chodorow's theories, the three different endings described by Dillon represent three different ways a daughter may attempt separation from her mother when she realizes that they are not one in the same body. In one version, "Gertrude drags Molly away," reflecting the daughter's fear, or wish, that through the power of the mother, separation may never occur. In the second version, "Molly runs out and kills herself," reflecting the daughter's fear that when separation does occur it will result in her death. In the published version, "Molly rushes off after Lionel," reflecting the Freudian scenario: daughter separates from mother through binding herself to a male figure. The fact that the play was produced on Broadway probably determined Bowles's choice of this last, least threatening to the heterosexual status quo, scenario. But its abruptness and the unfinished feelings it leaves are consistent with Chodorow's idea that for daughters this separation is experienced as arbitrary and never really complete. A feminist director could use an approach to production that stresses the play's lack of closure, perhaps by having Molly remain on the stage at the end or by using all three different endings in sequence.

The play also lends itself to examination through Rubin's ideas, which were discussed in chapter 3. Gertrude arranges for the exchange of herself to Mr. Solares as well as the exchange of Molly to Lionel, but since there is no father receiving some value in exchange for the women, the transaction is incomplete. The fact that these exchanges are not permanent causes the action of act 2; Gertrude returns to "take back" the daughter she had actually only "lent out" to Lionel in order to relieve herself of the anxiety of identifying with her. The implication is that the bond between mother and daughter transcends the exchange of marriage, even when the agent of exchange is the mother.

The power of the mother in the daughter's life is evident from the first moment of the play. Gertrude's larger-than-life aspect was emphasized in the original Broadway production by actress Judith Anderson (whose casting carried with it associations with Medea and other classical roles she had played). As the play begins Gertrude is seen up on a balcony overlooking the vine-covered summer house in which Molly sits—or, rather, hides. From a child's perspective, down in the womblike summer house, Gertrude is an overpowering presence.

In her opening "monologue" (actually a dialogue with infrequent responses from Molly), Gertrude realizes that Molly is, as usual, in the summer house: "If I believed in acts of violence, I would burn the summer house down."[37] She suspects Molly of "plotting." Molly has black hair, while Gertrude's is red. "Whenever I think of a woman going wild, I always picture her with black hair, never blond or red." Molly cannot picture women going wild, but her mother can: "They do it all the time. They break the bonds. . . . Sometimes I picture little scenes where they turn evil like wolves" (210). Gertrude suspects Molly of the violence within herself.

Men have no power to intervene in this mother-daughter dyad. Gertrude points out that Molly's father, now dead, was Spanish. "Spanish men aren't around the house much, which is a blessing. They're always out . . . sitting around with bunches of other men" (209). It is the same with Molly's Spanish stepfather, Mr. Solares, whom Gertrude marries in the course of the play. The action of the play charts Molly's struggle to deal with the alternating rejection and seduction she experiences from Gertrude. This push and pull between the two women is seen in startlingly naked form at several points.

The most painful moments occur in the last scene of act 1. Mother and daughter have gotten married in a double ceremony. As the scene opens, Molly is eating a hot dog and Gertrude has exchanged her shoes for bedroom slippers, but both women are still in their bridal gowns. The absence of the grooms until the leave-taking at the very end of the scene leaves the visual impression that the two brides have just married each other. This is the oedipal scene Freud could not envision: the daughter's desire to marry her first love object, her mother. But the daughter also feels the threat of separation. When Gertrude prepares to leave for Mexico, Molly hides again in the summer house and Gertrude addresses her from the balcony in the same words she used in the very beginning of the act:

Gertrude: Molly? Molly, are you in the summer house?
Molly: Yes, I am. (250)

The litany is followed by a new ending; Gertrude prepares to leave and Molly begs her to stay. Gertrude descends to the garden and Molly meets her with a bunch of honeysuckle, which Gertrude refuses to accept:

Molly: ...I picked them for you!

Gertrude: They're for your wedding. They belong to your dress. Here, put them back... [Bowles's ellipses]

Molly: No...No...They're for you...They're flowers for you!... I love you. I love you. Don't leave me. I love you. Don't go away! (252)

Molly's pathetic pleading rises to frenzy, but it only makes her mother more anxious to leave:

Gertrude: ...there's something heavy and dangerous inside you, like some terrible rock that's ready to explode....I can't bear it any more. I've got to get away, out of this garden. That's why I married. That's why I'm going away. I'm frightened of staying here with you any more. I can't breathe. (253)

Mother has married to escape daughter, while daughter has married to please, to imitate mother, to get closer rather than to escape. But daughter's efforts have failed and the dreaded separation occurs.

The contrasting pair of Mrs. Constable and her daughter Vivian can be seen as a different way of working out the daughter-mother ambivalence. Mrs. Constable gives unconditional love and cowers at the edges of her daughter's life. Vivian, however, feels the threat of merging with her mother and, as Chodorow has observed, fights against it by attaching herself to Gertrude. Her choice of Gertrude as object threatens Molly's less stable sense of self. Molly must kill, or feels she has killed, this threat. It is never made perfectly clear whether Molly killed Vivian or it was an accident. In either case, Molly feels guilt. One of the ironies of the play is that by the time Gertrude tries to use this "secret" to bind Molly to her at the end of the play, Mrs. Constable has become sympathetic toward Molly and does not want to hear the "secret." She has come to realize that Molly is like herself: "You're hanging on just like me. If she brought you her love you wouldn't know her" (273). In conversation with Gertrude a few minutes later, Mrs. Constable makes an analogy between Gertrude and herself: "How is Mrs. Lopez? If I were a man, I'd marry Mrs. Lopez. She'd be my type. We should both have been men. Two Spanish men, married to Mrs. Lopez" (277). The lines of identification and merging among the four women are subtle and complex.

Expanding the circle of relationships are Mrs. Lopez and her daughter, Frederica. With their warm, simple relationship and ease with each other, they serve as foils to the more neurotic WASPs. Bowles uses ethnic stereotypes in the play, stressing how noisy and happy the Mexican characters are. They are clearly portrayed as the "other" in relation to the white women. In a feminist production there are many spaces in the script in which these two characters could play a larger and more nuanced role in the action than the stage directions indicate. The contrasts and comparisons among the three pairs of mothers and daughters could be emphasized, perhaps indicating that all six are parts of one consciousness.

In summary, the characters of Molly and Vivian can be seen as the two sides of a daughter locked in ambivalent relationship with her first love object, her mother. As Chodorow summarizes, "A girl alternates between total rejection of a mother who represents infantile dependence [Vivian] and attachment to her [Molly], between identification with anyone other than her mother [Vivian] and feeling herself her mother's double and extension [Molly]." This bonding, of course, goes both ways: "Her mother often mirrors her preoccupations."[38] In the play, Mrs. Constable has Molly's mode of operating (attachment) and Gertrude has more of Vivian's (rejection). Each daughter seems to have the inappropriate mother for her needs. The presence of Mrs. Lopez and Frederica seems to offer an ideal the other pairs cannot approach.

The seriousness, complexity, and centrality of the daughter's struggle against and engagement with her mother in this play surpass the mother-daughter portrayals in any canonized American drama. Amanda and Laura in *The Glass Managerie* are the one pair that entered the canon, but the engagement between them is more observed than felt. *In the Summer House* did not enter the canon and has not led to a tradition of dangerous and explosive woman-written, felt-from-the-inside plays about mothers and daughters. Sue-Ellen Case's remarks on medieval woman playwright Hrotsvit's place in the history of drama apply to some degree to Bowles's as well: "Contemporary women's plays are more likely to be excluded from the canon because there is no precedent or tradition of development towards them and the position of the pioneer is excluded because there is no tradition of development which springs from her initial model."[39] Bowles's play is important and should be more widely known through production, anthologizing, and scholarly work.

Yet increasing the number and authenticity of stage portrayals of female characters may not solve an underlying problem. Even as we work toward having more female authors and characters, we need to consider the question of the representation of women. It is possible to put women, and not just "Woman," on the stage? Is the entire apparatus of theater so male-conceived and dominated that women cannot be "seen" through it? These are some of the questions feminist film theorists have already raised. Feminists in theater need to pay attention to these underlying questions as well.

CHAPTER 5

Feminist Film Theory: "Man as Bearer of the Look" and the Representation of Women

Semiotics

Feminist film theorists began analyzing the construction of gender on the screen almost fifteen years earlier than feminist theater theorists began examining gender on the stage. The large body of existing film theory is an obvious source for thinking about the representation of women on the stage, though some changes need to be made due to qualities of live performance. One of the basic methods for film analysis, psychosemiotics, combines insights from psychoanalysis (particularly Lacan's) with those from the field of semiotics; it analyzes the relationship of film to individual identity through, among other techniques, a very close reading of all the elements present in each frame of film.

Semiotics is the study of signs, each of which is composed of a signifier and a signified. Sue-Ellen Case gives the following definitions: "The signifier is the ensemble of elements in a theatrical production that compose its meaning—the text, the actor, the stage space, the lights, the blocking, and so on. The signified is the meaning or message which is derived from this signifier by the 'collective consciousness' of the audience."[1] The sign is separate from the referent, or "real" object for which the sign stands. One of the important things about semiotics for feminism, according to Case, is its focus on the "cultural encoding of the sign" or "the imprint of ideology upon the sign—the set of values, beliefs and ways of seeing that control the connotations of the sign in the culture at large" (116). Each object, body, and gesture on stage is inscribed with cultural meanings, and semiotics helps focus analysis on the fact that these signs are not value-free. Feminist semiotics examines "woman as sign," finds that "woman" is a cultural construct, and attempts to deconstruct this sign, "in order to distinguish biology from culture and experience from ideology. Whereas formerly feminist criticism presumed to know what a woman is, but rejected certain images of women, this new perspective brings into question the entire notion of how one knows what the sign 'woman' means" (118).

Semiotics has a long history, going back to the Prague School structuralists and early work in linguistics. Keir Elam has outlined this history in the first book that brought together the ideas of semiotics and applied them to theater and drama, and since 1980 a number of other writers have contributed books on various aspects of the relationship of semiotics to theater.[2]

Most theater semiotic work has not been feminist, while the major object of feminist semiotic scrutiny has been film. Most of the third-stage feminist performance criticism mentioned in chapter 1 is an exception to this. A particularly good example is an essay by Case, in which she says that in recent plays by women playwrights, three types of "subject positions emerge: the split subject, the metonymically displaced subject, and the collective subject."[3] Examples of plays in each of the categories are *Getting Out,* by Marsha Norman, *India Song,* by Marguerite Duras, and *Beauty and the Beast,* by Split Britches.

A good introduction to feminist psychosemiotics, using films as objects of analysis, is Kaja Silverman's *The Subject of Semiotics.* Silverman gives some history of semiotics, as well as background in philosophy and psychology on the "subject." As she says, the term *subject* "helps us to conceive of human reality as a construction, as the product of signifying activities, which are both culturally specific and generally unconscious. . . . [It] calls into question the notions both of the private, and of a self synonymous with consciousness."[4] In her chapter titled "The Subject," Silverman discusses the stages the male subject goes through, according to Freud and Lacan, but in addition states that she will "endeavor to create a space for the female subject within these pages, even if that space is only a negative one—one, that is, which reflects the marginality to which she has been confined for centuries" (131).

Silverman describes the Freudian model of male development in which the child passes through the oral, anal, and oedipal stages, with focus on the differences in the ways male and female children react to the differences in their anatomies. Freud "privileges" the penis and has the female subject define herself by its lack. This binary opposition extends to other traits as well: "He associates the male subject with aggressivity, voyeurism, and sadism, and the female subject with the antithetical but complementary qualities of passivity, exhibitionism, and masochism" (138).

In the Lacanian model, Silverman points out four stages: "the subject's birth and the zoning of its body. . . . the mirror stage, the acquisition of language, and the adventures of the Oedipal" (151). Lacan says that "between the ages of six months and eighteen months the subject arrives at an apprehension of both its self and the other—indeed, of its self *as other*. This discovery is assisted by the child seeing, for the first time, its own reflection in a mirror" (157). But the reflection is a "mis-recognition," and the subject knows it. "It loves the coherent identity which the mirror provides. However, because the image remains external to it, it also hates that image" (158). The analogies of mirror with film become clearer and clearer. But the construction of sexual difference is a large part of what goes on in this mirror stage, and, as in Freud, the female subject is inadequately theorized. At the end of the chapter, Silverman cautions that the models of Freud and Lacan must be read actively, not passively, if they are to be used to help develop a feminist psychosemiotics. "Turned around upon themselves, these models can even help us to conceive of a different signification, a different subjectivity, and a different symbolic order" (192). The finding of this different order is much of the work of feminist film theory.

Feminist Film Theory Surveyed

Film theory in general has developed along lines very different from those of theater. Feminist theory is probably more fully developed in film than elsewhere because of the strong theoretical orientation of the film field. Britain in the early 1970s had already started producing third-stage feminist film theory around the same time the United States produced the books I have already mentioned as being first-stage: *Popcorn Venus* (1973) and *From Reverence to Rape* (1974). However, a 1976 British overview essay mentions only those two books and one other before going on to point out their shortcomings and recommending new directions for feminist film criticism. The writers reflect the socialist-feminist view of many British women writing about film.:

> In summary, then, it is in three areas that we feel feminist criticism must become articulate: a historical-economic analysis of our society, an awareness of the broad range of possibilities in the relationship between art and ideology, and a grasp of the visual as well as narrative language of film.[5]

Two years later, Christine Gledhill wrote a much more detailed overview, summarizing the British socialist-feminist work that had appeared to that point in journals such as *Screen, Camera Obscura, Women and Film,* and *Jump Cut*. The main theorist-critics she considers are Claire Johnston, Pam Cook, and Laura Mulvey. The essay is useful in that it summarizes ideas of three main theorists whose work is applied to film theory: Roland Barthes (semiotics), Althusser (Marxism), and Lacan (psychoanalysis). This detailed picture of where feminist film criticism was in 1978 seems light-years ahead of where feminist theater criticism is over a decade later. Gledhill virtually negates the possibility of first- and second-stage criticism:

> For our purposes there are two questions: What is the relation of women to language as speaking subject? What is the role of the representation of women in cultural artifacts? Put simply: Can women speak, and can images of women speak for women? The answers seem negative.[6]

Gledhill shows how feminist film criticism has shifted focus from content to form and mechanism of films, and discusses the relation of these forms to ideology. She does see some dangers:

> The ultimate problem, it seems to me, lies in the attempt to make language and the signifying process so exclusively central

to the production of the social formation. Under the insistence on the semiotic production of meaning, the effectivity of social, economic, and political practice threatens to disappear altogether. . . . to say that language has a determining effect on society is a different matter from saying that society is nothing but its languages and signifying practices.[7]

In 1985 Judith Mayne declared in her review essay in *Signs:* "It is only a slight exaggeration to say that most feminist film theory and criticism of the last decade has been a response, implicit or explicit, to the issues raised in Laura Mulvey's article."[8] Mayne summarizes work in the previously mentioned three methodologies used in film theory: semiotics, Marxism, and psychoanalysis:

Central to each is an issue of representation. According to the semioticians, film was to be understood as a systematic network of binary oppositions, organized metaphorically, if not literally, like language. Marxists, especially those influenced by the work of Louis Althusser, stressed that ideology was a function of representation, and the function of film as an ideological medium would be evaluated in terms of its forms of address to the spectator. And psychoanalytic critics, particularly those following Jacques Lacan, insisted that the look, and therefore the structure of point of view, was central in filmic identification, here understood as an imaginary coherence of the subject. (85)

Mayne stresses not trying to reconcile all the contradictions in the field, but rather trying to examine the tensions and to "rethink dualism itself" (86). Pointing toward the future, she mentions the trend of "understanding film in a more broadly cultural sense" and trying "to get beyond dualistic categories while understanding their power to attract" (99).

Though a large amount of the most important work in feminist film theory has, since the early 1970s, appeared in periodicals, beginning in 1973 a number of anthologies of essays were published.[9] One of the earliest was *Women in Film Noir,* edited by E. Ann Kaplan,[10] a collection of original essays on the *noir* form of Hollywood's 1940s and 1950s. Contributors such as Christine Gledhill, Pam Cook, and Claire Johnston did close psychoanalytic-socialist-feminist readings of individual films and drew some general conclusions about the ambiguity for feminists of this film form in which dangerous women are so prominent.

Another anthology, *Re-vision,* contains three essays previously published (by Gledhill, Mayne, and B. Ruby Rich) and four (by Kaja Silverman, Teresa de Lauretis, and editors Doane and Williams) that were given at a conference in 1981 and then revised. The introduction by the editors gives a chronology of the feminist film movement and an overview of the split within the critical part of that movement between "essentialists" and "anti-essentialists." As the editors point out:

> One can thus trace a marked movement within feminist [film] theory over the past decade from an analysis of difference as oppressive to a delineation and specification of difference as liberating, as offering the only possibility of radical change. However, the dangers of such a valorization of femininity as difference or heterogeneity are clear.[11]

The dilemma of "the dangers of essentialism" versus what I call "Where do you start if you don't say women are different from men?" is a constant subject in feminist film theory. As Judith Mayne points out, the differences between these views have "hardened into the same kind of dualistic opposition as that separating the classical Hollywood cinema from its alternatives," and "the both-and of *woman* and *women* is a far more productive situating of the feminist enterprise than the either-or of essentialism and antiessentialism."[12] This essentialism debate is also an active one among feminist theater critics.

However, even without the resolution of this dilemma, many useful insights gained from film work are applicable to theater. For instance, the editors of *Re-vision* point out as one of the limits of "image" criticism that "in film even the most blatant stereotype is naturalized by a medium that presents a convincing illusion of a flesh and blood woman."[13] In theater the stereotype is naturalized *by* a flesh and blood woman. The examination of live actors as "signs" is part of theatrical semiotics.

In the 1980s three books by single authors (Annette Kuhn, E. Ann Kaplan, and Teresa de Lauretis) have had influence on the field. *Women's Pictures,* by Annette Kuhn,[14] relates feminism and film through two major tasks: part 3 is titled "Rereading Dominant Cinema: Feminism and Film Theory," and part 4 is called "Replacing Dominant Cinema: Feminism and Film Practice." This book in effect combines a third-stage approach with the tasks of first- and second-stage criticism, summarizing previous work and applying Kuhn's own amalgamation to some specific films. A review of the book in *Camera Obscura*, like many such reviews in feminist publications, carries on a dialogue with the book, agreeing and disagreeing, describing and criticizing:

> Kuhn eliminates very little from the purview of her topic. She covers the field of film theory, notes remaining problems, calls for additional work to expand the outer limits of feminist theory, and perceives from a "meta-level" the implications of putting together the components of her book: feminism and cinema, theory and practice, feminist and non-feminist contemporary theory. One reads with the impression that she has answered all possible inconsistencies, stopped up every logical hole. The style of the book is precise, reasoned, and well-orchestrated.
>
> Commendable as these attributes are, they contribute to an overall problem: the clarity of the book is, in some places, deceptive. Genuine difficulties in the literature and politics of Kuhn's subject get glossed over.[15]

Kuhn continues to write—both articles and a book of essays have been published since *Women's Pictures*.[16]

Published the year after Kuhn's book, E. Ann Kaplan's *Women and Film*[17] is similar in some respects. Kaplan also divides her book into two sections: "The Classical and Contemporary Hollywood Cinema" and "The Independent Feminist Film." Her first chapter asks in its title the key question "Is the Gaze Male?" and answers in the affirmative for most Hollywood films. She quotes Laura Mulvey, substituting "gaze" for "look," to the effect that these films construct male subjects gazing at female objects on three levels: characters within the film, the camera's "eye," and spectators looking at the film. A large portion of her book is devoted to close, "against the grain" (similar to "resisting") reading of specific films. Her particular interest is the representation of motherhood and the use of that theme to approach films in a feminist manner. Kaplan's book has stirred debate, and she has replied to criticisms about it being on the wrong side of the essentialist question, though it is perceived as being both pro and con, depending on the critic read.[18]

The third influential book published in the 1980s is Teresa de Lauretis's *Alice Doesn't: Feminism, Semiotics, Cinema.*[19] In a series of six essays she touches on many theorists in a wide range of fields, but there is little defining or summarizing. This is a book for people who are already more than a little familiar with semiotics and psychoanalysis, and for that reason it is more difficult to follow than the others. For instance, from her introduction:

> The second project of this work is to confront those texts and discourses with feminist theory and *its* articulation of what is at issue in cultural notions of femininity, the working of desire in narrative, the configurations of affective investment in cinematic identification and spectatorship, or the mutual overdetermination of meaning, perception and experience.[20]

An especially interesting aspect of the book is the chapter "Desire in Narrative," in which de Lauretis relates narrative to the oedipal complex and to sexual difference. Her work is too complex to summarize here, but leads the way toward the most sophisticated theorization going on today. De Lauretis has subsequently published articles, edited an anthology, and published a book of essays that further develop her theory.[21]

Other single-author books published since 1985 have continued to extend the discussion of feminist film theory. *Film Feminisms,* by Mary C. Gentile,[22] summarizes feminist and nonfeminist film theories and does not fear being "prescriptive" by offering suggestions for future directions for feminist film theory. *The Pornography of Representation,* by Susanne Kappeler,[23] on the other hand, is divided into thirteen "problems" and addresses itself to both the narrower topic of pornography and the broader topic to which all the other writers have addressed themselves: the representation of women in film. Other 1980s books have dealt with the genre of the "woman's film," the female voice in film, the films of Alfred Hitchcock, and the relation of the avant-garde and popular culture.[24] Several anthologies have offered a cross-section of the most important essays from past and present, pointing toward the current feminist interest in topics such as popular culture and theorizing the female spectator, or "female gaze."[25]

Feminist film theory continues to be written, but it is time for theater to use some of these same ideas in relation to both drama and live performance. One way to begin is to consider the germinal essay cited more often than any other, that of Laura Mulvey.

Laura Mulvey and "Man as Bearer of the Look"

Mulvey is both a theoretician and a filmmaker, and her writing style is relatively accessible. That she successfully summarized a number of rather complex theories and inserted the issue of gender into the discussion generated by male film theorists probably accounts for the extensive citation by other critics of her 1975 article "Visual Pleasure and Narrative Cinema."[26] Like Gayle Rubin's in anthropology, Mulvey's article seems an Ur-text in the field of feminist film theory and criticism, especially for those who favor the psychoanalytic approach. Even those who oppose such an approach use Mulvey's article as the thesis with which to disagree. Its appearance rather early on in the chronology of feminist theorizing also helped make it the text with which to reckon.

Mulvey says at the very beginning of her introduction that she is using psychoanalytic theory "as a political weapon, demonstrating the way the unconscious of patriarchal society has structured film form" (361). In her second paragraph she summarizes psychoanalysis as it applies to cinema: "The function of woman in forming the patriarchal unconscious is twofold; she first symbolizes the castration threat by her real absence of a penis and second thereby raises her child into the symbolic" (361). After a little more explanation she admits that psychoanalysis is itself a tool of patriarchy, but defends its use for studying the status quo in order to break out of it. She also anticipates many of her critics by listing some of the things she will not be dealing with: "the sexing of the female infant and her relationship to the symbolic, the sexually mature woman as nonmother, maternity outside the signification of the phallus, the vagina ..." (362). She is once again clear about her aim: "It is said that analyzing pleasure, or beauty, destroys it. That is the intention of this essay. . . . to make way for a total negation of the ease and plenitude of the narrative fiction film" (363).

In the second section, "Pleasure in Looking—Fascination with the Human Form," Mulvey explains Freud's notion of scopophilia, or "the voyeuristic activities of children, their desire to see and make sure of the private and the forbidden . . . genital and bodily functions, about the presence or absence of the penis" (363). She summarizes some nonfeminist film theory that links watching film with this scopophilic pleasure, the magic world that unwinds in the light while the audience is at a distance in the dark, looking at it. She then describes the Lacanian mirror stage and the narcissism that results from the child seeing its own image reflected. In short, the "two contradictory aspects of the pleasurable structures of looking in the conventional cinematic situation" are the scopophilic, which "arises from pleasure in using another person as an object of sexual stimulation through sight," and the narcissistic, which "comes from identification with the image seen" (365).

In section 3, "Woman as Image, Man as Bearer of the Look," she goes on to show how, for the male spectator, scopophilia and narcissism lead to the objectification of the female and identification with the male protagonist on screen. The woman as object works on two levels: "as erotic object for the characters within the screen story, and as erotic object for the spectator within the auditorium." Because "the male figure cannot bear the burden of sexual objectification," the protagonist is usually male and has the role of "forwarding the story, making things happen" (367). And in order to deal with the male audience's castration anxiety, the female object is either devalued, punished, or saved; or turned into a fetish. Mulvey then uses examples from the work of Joseph von Sternberg and Hitchcock to clearly and convincingly demonstrate her points.

In her summary, she admits that the psychoanalytic explanation of the representation of woman she has discussed is not intrinsic to film, but that, unlike theater's objectification of woman,

> cinema builds the way she is to be looked at into the spectacle itself. Playing on the tension between film as controlling the dimension of time (editing, narrative) and film as controlling the dimension of space (changes in distance, editing), cinematic codes create a gaze, a world, and an object, thereby producing an illusion cut to the measure of desire. It is these cinematic codes and their relationship to formative external structures that must be broken down before mainstream film and the pleasure it provides can be challenged. (372–73)

The voyeuristic "look" that she has described can be further broken down into three forms: "that of the camera as it records the profilmic event, that of the audience as it watches the final product, and that of the characters at each other within the screen illusion." Narrative film tries to "deny the first two and subordinate them to the third," to prevent "a distancing awareness in the audience." Mulvey ends with a call to "free the look of the camera into its materiality in time and space and the look of the audience into dialectics, passionate detachment" (373). Though this may destroy pleasure, it is a necessary destruction for women.

Although Mulvey stresses that these theories are uniquely applicable to film, they are clearly adaptable to theater as well. Much of her call for "passionate detachment" in the audience sounds exactly like Brecht. But Mulvey deals with the specificity of women in a way Brecht did not and gives many useful ideas for the feminist criticism of theater as well as for the writing of plays. Scopophilia and narcissism are just as actively at work in live performance as in film, perhaps more today than in earlier decades because of the use of filmic devices on the stage. The objectification of women and use of predominantly male protagonists in dramatic literature is certainly as true as for film. What theater lacks is the fine-tuned control of the camera's "look," though certain theatrical devices related to framing, lighting, costume, foregrounding, and interruption can perform some of the same functions. Some of Mulvey's ideas are especially applicable to plays written in the 1980s, which consciously foreground issues of representation. However, they are also applicable to some plays written during a period of great activity in nonmainstream theater as well as in film theory, the late 1960s to early 1970s.

Sam Shepard's *The Tooth of Crime*

The Tooth of Crime, first performed in 1972, is "A Play with Music in Two Acts."[27] Act 1 presents Hoss, an aging rock star in the sci-fi future who senses that a younger challenger will come to fight him for his turf. Surrounded by one female, Becky, and four male helpers, Hoss anticipates this rival and by the end of the act he has arrived, offstage, in the form of Crow. Act 2 is almost entirely devoted to stages of the struggle between the two singers for dominance, culminating in a final "shoot-out." They fight using various self-images, then go three rounds in a refereed "bout" of speak-singing and intimidation. Crow wins these rounds and forces Hoss to exchange personae with him. Then Crow presents Hoss with a girl who uses her own hands to act out backseat petting and will not let Hoss go "all the way" with her, and in a vulnerable condition Hoss is led to a moment of self-recognition by Crow and shoots himself. Crow is the victor and takes over the territory, with the implication that the cycle of challenge and defeat will continue endlessly.

The play contains many of Shepard's frequent preoccupations: the American West, jazz and rock music, male domains such as cars and sports, two male figures exchanging personae, and the oedipal struggle between father and son figures. The overall structure is amazingly oedipal, in fact, but with Laius pushed onstage and Jocasta, as she so often is, pushed off. Songs punctuate the action at frequent intervals, functioning often like Greek choral interludes. The moment of self-discovery near the end leads directly to self-destruction. But an interesting point is that the figure of Hoss is the central son figure, whose story we follow, turned into father figure through the appearance of a son, with no necessity of a wife or mother at all.

Mulvey's ideas of scopophilia and narcissism can easily be applied to this play, showing the similarities and differences between their operation in film and on the stage vis-à-vis women. In all Shepard's plays there is at least one male protagonist, encouraging male narcissistic identification, and rarely more than one or two women, who are always in subsidiary roles. Shepard's women are at least as often, in Mulvey's terms, "devalued" as they are "fetishized" or made into objects for the male look. But Shepard's main emphasis is on creation of male protagonists who are strongly engaged with each other.

Shepard's plays of the 1960s and 1970s often resemble some films of that period that did not contain a female sexual object because, as Mulvey says, the female tends to "freeze the flow of action in moments of erotic contemplation." Mulvey goes on, parenthetically:

(A recent tendency in narrative film has been to dispense with this problem altogether; hence the development of what Molly Haskell has called the "buddy movie," in which the active homo-sexual eroticism of the central male figures can carry the story without distraction.) (366)

Though Shepard does use some female figures, his are essentially "buddy plays," with emphasis on male homosocial relationships, similar to most plays of O'Neill and Miller. Shepard turns O'Neill's whore and Miller's wife into a trivial secretary/gofer/girlfriend during this period of his plays, though later he does admit a few daughters and mothers into his "family" plays.

Sometimes there is a connection between homosocial behavior and homosexual baiting. The three "wins" in the play on the part of Crow are all achieved by attacking Hoss's masculinity. In round 1, Crow wins by piling words upon words, most with homosexual associations, from "catch ya' with yer pants down. Whip ya' with a belt. . . . Leave ya' cryin' for Ma" (237) to:

> In the slammer he's a useless. . . . Turns into a candy-cock just to get a reprieve. . . . Finally gets his big chance and sucks the warden's dinger. . . . Just gimme some head boy. Just get down on your knees. Gimme some blow big boy. I'll give ya' back the key. (238)

Round 3 is also won by Crow, with lines ranging from "Still gets a hard on but can't get it up" (242) to:

> Wearin' a shag now, looks like a fag now. Can't get it together with chicks in the mag. . . . Busted and bleedin' all over the floor. All bleedin' and wasted and tryin' to score. (243)

The third "hit" comes when Crow tells Hoss, "Empty your head." The image that appears on stage is Becky:

> She wears a black wig and is dressed like Anna Karina in "Alphaville." She caresses herself as though her hands were a man's, feeling her tits, her thighs, her waist. Sometimes when one hand seems to take too much advantage she seizes it with the other hand and pushes it away. (247)

The image this stage direction presents is that of a divided woman subject entirely fetishized and presented as an object to be looked at. She keeps up a monologue, trying to placate the "man" whose hands are her own.

Stage directions set up the fetish: *"Becky* talks straight out to the audience. But directs it at *Hoss."* After a bit of talk, "her hands pull off her sweater. The wig comes off with it. She's wearing a stiff white bra underneath." She says, "I'm not that kind of a girl"; then "her hands rip off her bra and feel her tits." She tries to talk about his car, but "her hands unzip her skirt and tear it off. One hand tries to get inside her panties while the other hand fights it off." She says "I don't wanna go all the way. I'm not that kind of a girl. . . . Let me out!" Having no actual man to contend with, she easily makes her escape: "She picks up her clothes and runs off." After this, Hoss says he feels "trapped. Defeated. Shot down" (248). From this position, it is easy for Crow to get Hoss to "vision" himself as a Crow-like, "pitiless" figure, the recognition of which sends him into suicidal despair.

The stage image of a woman "feeling up" her own body is a powerful one. As Mulvey says, she acts as an erotic object for both the male characters and spectators. But in having the woman perform the actions upon herself, Shepard also conveys the message that the woman is responsible for being attacked by the man; she does it to herself. The man is but the poor recipient of her rejection. He is "shot down" by her, not by his male rival. She gives pleasure, then snatches it away. But the male in the audience identifies with Hoss's downfall and achieves catharsis, or may identify with Crow and feel victorious. The female in the audience is left to identify against herself, once again, having never received anything but unpleasure from the woman on the stage.

Alice Childress's *Wine in the Wilderness*

In her play *Wine in the Wilderness* (1969), black playwright Alice Childress acts as a feminist critic through both the play itself and the character Tommorrow Marie (Tommy). Childress portrays a black male painter who produces stereotypical images of black women on canvas, but learns to modify those images drastically through the example of Tommy.

In the aftermath of a racial riot in Harlem, a black liberal couple (Sonny-Man and Cynthia) bring Tommy, a thirty-year-old factory worker, to the apartment of Bill, a slightly older painter, to serve as a model for the final panel of a triptych he is painting called "Wine in the Wilderness." Before Tommy's arrival, Bill explains to his friend, Oldtimer, that the paintings portray three aspects of "black womanhood": chaste "black girlhood," majestic "Mother Africa," and the as yet unpainted "lost woman," represented on the stage by a blank canvas. Tommy is attracted to Bill and stays overnight with him, but when she finds out the kind of painting he had planned, she tells him that he likes "Afro-Americans" in the abstract but that "you don't like flesh and blood niggers."[28] By then Bill has come to realize that women like Tommy are indeed the "Wine in the Wilderness" he thought he was painting. He plans to change the triptych to one in which Tommy as she is forms the central panel, with Oldtimer on one side and the liberal couple on the other side, "workin' together to do our thing" (421).

Childress dramatizes male scopophilia through showing a man in the act of trying to objectify "black womanhood," particularly in the early scene in which Bill shows his paintings to Oldtimer and in Bill's early relations with Tommy. When Bill uncovers the "Wine in the Wilderness" canvas, he reveals a beautiful woman "draped in startling colors of African material, very *Vogue* looking. She wears a golden head-dress sparkling with brilliants and sequins applied over the paint." He says, "Mother Africa, regal, black womanhood in her noblest form" (387). When he uncovers the empty canvas, Oldtimer says, "Your . . . your pitcher is gone." Bill explains he has yet to paint that canvas, but when he does it will be

> the lost woman, . . . what the society has made out of our women. She's as far from my African queen as a woman can get and still be female, she's as close to the bottom as you can get without crackin' up . . . she's ignorant, unfeminine, coarse, rude . . . vulgar . . . a poor, dumb chick that's had her behind kicked until it's numb . . . and the sad part is . . . she ain't together, you know, . . . there's no hope for her. [Childress's ellipses]

Later he adds, "If you had to sum her up in one word it would be nothin'!" (388). Then he covers the empty canvas. But he is not going to allow an empty canvas to represent this "nothin'" woman. He is going to paint the "chick" his friends are bringing to the apartment. "When she gets put down on canvas, . . . then triptych will be finished" (389).

When Tommy does arrive, Bill tries to keep her within the frame he has constructed for her, but she jumps out. When he is alone with her for the first time, he makes a series of pronouncements about black women:

"That's the trouble with our women, yall always got your mind on food" (402); "Trouble with our women, . . . they all wanta be great brains" (405); "Our women don't know a damn thing 'bout bein' feminine" (406); and "That's another thing with our women, . . . they wanta *latch* on" (407). All these statements are clearly contradicted by Tommy's behavior in the play, but it takes Bill a while to get that message.

After Tommy has removed her wig and mismatched clothes snatched up during the riot, she has a more "natural" appearance, which is not the image Bill wants to paint. He tries to get her to put the wig back on but she refuses. He asks her to start talking, and she tells him some of her history and that of the Black Elks organization, surprising Bill with her background and knowledge. He gives up painting that night and decides instead to sleep with Tommy. She is more than willing, but when she learns the truth from Oldtimer about Bill's intended painting of her the next morning she strikes out at the betrayal of her trust just as Bill is changing his mind about her. She tells Bill off and let's him know for sure that "I don't have to wait for anybody's by-your-leave to be a 'Wine In The Wilderness' woman. I can be it if I wanta, . . . and I *am,* I am. I am. I'm not the one you made up and painted, the very pretty lady who can't talk back" (419). Tommy does not allow Bill to devalue, punish, save, or fetishize her. The female "muse" resists being "written" as what she is not and acts as a critic, before the fact, influencing the making of the art in a more active way than that of a passive model. She inserts "I am" into the picture.

The play seems to begin with a male protagonist, Bill, but as soon as Tommy appears onstage she is clearly a protagonist as well. She is the one responsible for "making things happen" in the play and Bill is the one who undergoes change. The double-protagonist structure gives both female and male audience members an active subject on the stage with which to identify if they wish to do so. There is no manipulation of the audience to identify with one gender at the expense of constructing the other as an object. There is in this play, unlike so many by male authors, a scene between women, between Tommy and Cynthia, in which Cynthia realizes long before Bill does that the actual Tommy is not the image they had preconstructed of her. Tommy raises Cynthia's consciousness by sharing her experiences, which strike a note of recognition in Cynthia. This scene points out that race and gender liberation are separate but related pursuits for black women. The scene is permeated by a sense of the honesty possible between women when they are not looked at by men. Such a scene is almost nonexistent in plays that do not portray women as active subjects. There is a power in women getting together that is dangerous to male dominance.

The fact that this is a play with black characters based in black experience makes identification with it simpler for black audience members than for white ones. Like all black drama, it puts whites in the unfamiliar position of making the "adjustment" to seeing characters not of their own race on the stage. At the same time, the play does not have the radical racial message of many black plays of the late 1960s. Childress critiqued false Afro-American separatist rhetoric that was not accompanied by genuine feeling and action. A black audience in 1969 may have had to make its own "adjustment" to her message.

The sign of "Woman" in this play bears the double cultural encoding of black in a white-dominant culture and female in a male-dominant one. The difference in this play is that the sign speaks about the fact that there is a difference between what is signified to the others and what is signified to Tommy by Tommy's body. It is difficult to misinterpret a sign that speaks so forcefully of its signification. Several characters comment on the differences between Bill's image for the original painting and the reality of Tommy. Oldtimer says, "It's art, . . . it's only art. . . . He couldn't mean you," (414) and Cynthia adds, "Tommy, we didn't know you" (415). Then Tommy makes her own analysis: "I was Tommin' to you, to all of you, . . . 'Oh, maybe they gon' like me.' . . . I was your fool, thinkin' writers and painters know moren' me" (416).

The sign of the blank canvas signifies both the lack of black female images and the vast potential to be realized by future works like the one at hand. It is also a highly theatrical image with many production possibilities attached. Plays like this one put the power of shaping the signifier in the hands of black women, where it has rarely been, and where the potential for radical signification is great.

Looking at these two plays through Mulvey's ideas points up the fact that "Woman" on stage has most often been constructed by men, to be viewed by other men as an object. Feminist production of plays like Shepard's can use the means already discussed, such as cross-gender casting, to emphasize gender issues and to subvert the usual functioning of the "look." Increased production of plays like Childress's, which are a critique of representation in themselves, could lead to a tradition of women writing plays that question the images men have constructed. There are many ways that a feminist critique of representation might appear on the stage, some of which are just now beginning to be produced.

CHAPTER 6

Moving Ahead

This journey through feminist theory is far from an end, but it has reached some preliminary destinations. I have shown the usefulness of applying feminist theories to drama, the untapped source of material that theater offers to women's studies, the broad spectrum of feminist approaches that are possible, and what I hope is a cogent argument for the use of theory itself for feminist purposes. The various political perspectives on feminism, as well as black and lesbian feminism, can make great contributions to sharpening the tools of theories drawn from academic fields such as literary criticism, anthropology, psychology, and film theory. Work needs to continue on all three stages of feminist criticism, while continuing on into others as well.

Let me be prescriptive for one moment. I feel that some awareness of feminist theory on the part of critics, directors, designers, actors, and playwrights should encourage the writing and production of more plays written strongly from women's points of view. This is not to say that all plays by or about women need be stimulated by feminist theory, but the stimulation itself might yield surprising results. Still, this is no "take two and call me in the morning" prescription, since there is hardly any agreement on what the "two" taken should be. The wider dissemination of ideas and the opening up of possibilities that include women as active subjects are what I am advocating.

I cannot call this last chapter "conclusion," because not only is there so much yet to be done that I could not use the word, but there is no single conclusion to be drawn about feminist dramatic criticism in mid-1990. I can say that in my experience it is easiest to apply feminist literary criticism to the written play and feminist film theory to performance, but that "conclusion" merely restates the obvious and does not push the field to go beyond. It may ultimately be more revealing to use the theories in exactly the opposite configuration. The fields of social science seem about equally applicable to both drama and performance. My biggest conclusion is that just about everything remains to be done and the prospects for just that are very exciting.

In looking toward future work in this field there are so many remaining possibilities: fields from which to draw theories and plays to which to apply them. In arriving at the academic fields to survey for this book, I became acutely aware of the many I was not able to include. Feminist explorations in philosophy, political science, sociology, and history were barely touched upon, but they have much to offer, especially in methodology. Other fields not even mentioned include science, linguistics, narratology, art, dance, and music, each of which is amassing its own growing literature of feminist theory. I concerned myself mainly with American theorists, but many other countries are contributing important ideas toward global feminist theorizing.

The field of plays to which all theories could be applied should be broadened. Some work has been done on Ibsen, the Greeks, and particularly Shakespeare, but other periods and countries could be approached from a feminist theoretical standpoint. The study of these plays needs to be in all three stages of feminist criticism: images of women, women as writers, and a broader theoretical approach that may lead to fourth and fifth stages. The nineteenth and early twentieth centuries are especially ripe for elucidation of female images and women playwrights, many of whom are almost ignored in both criticism and history of theater.

The contributions of radical and materialist feminist theory—how they differ from each other as well as from liberal contributions—need further investigation. Liberal feminism in relation to theater also needs to be explored. Finally, all this work needs to be applied to all production aspects of theater as well as to the texts themselves. As I have indicated, some theorists are going in this direction, especially in third-stage work and in relation to performance art. But the impact of feminist theory in areas such as the history of acting or the feminist implications of theater architecture has yet to be felt and could be considerable.

That most of dramatic history has constructed inaccurate and damaging representations of women does not mean that the trend should continue, unbalanced by women. There is little reason to hope that representations will improve unless feminist women themselves criticize the existing structures and counter them. Women audiences and practitioners have much at stake in seeing that such images do change. Men barely realize the difference that more equitable representation of women would have on them as well. Through pointing out that theater is a frame, not a mirror, and through using theater as a laboratory for deconstructing the old and constructing new representations of women, theater can be changed.

In the end, I say that working in feminist theory has been an enormous influence in my own life and work. I have discovered fresh inspiration for writing about and teaching drama and theater through being able to incorporate realities with which I can now identify. I have also found that paying attention to women is a complex process that can give intense pleasure. Philosopher Marilyn Frye has written the best description I have found: "Attention is a kind of passion. When one's attention is on something, one is present in a particular way with respect to that thing. This presence is, among other things, an element of erotic presence."[1] In some way related to the presence of "the look" articulated in film theory is what I would call the "erotics of theory." When the subject of scrutiny is women, perhaps due to preoedipal factors, the attention is indeed "a kind of passion." I have felt that passion in reading feminist theories, in feeling theorists' engagement with their subject and with each other, and in reading and seeing plays in performance through a feminist lens.

This passion has led to my desire to share the workings of feminist criticism with others and, to do so, my adoption of a performative stance toward feminist theory and criticism. Film critic Tania Modleski has written about the function of feminist criticism as being, in anthropological terms, "in the realm of symbolic exchange—the realm, that is, of the gift," that is, symbolic exchange "between the critic and the women to whom she talks and writes." She goes on to say that feminist criticism may "have a performative dimension—i.e., to be *doing* something beyond restating already existent ideas and views." It can become a speech act, in J. L. Austin's terms.[2] In my case, passion has become an urge to create performative acts in the form of feminist "theory plays."

In the course of writing this book I have turned back to my earlier interest, playwriting, and stepped into the laboratory of theater with my own experiment. Inspired by Judith Fetterley's work on Hawthorne's "The Birthmark" (see chap. 2), I compiled and directed *Resisting the Birth Mark*. A cast of four females and one male switch roles throughout, portraying two feminist critics, scientist Aylmer, wife Georgiana, and the visible stage manager, while a male tape-recorded voice reads sections of Hawthorne's narration of the story. In ten short scenes I juxtaposed narrative and dialogue from the story with brief segments of feminist theory and sections that disrupted the narrative. For example, near the end, "Georgiana" takes the potion and reclines on a table. While narration is heard from the tape recorder, "Aylmer" goes to an overhead projector located in the audience area and uses it to "draw" with red marker on the female body on the table. As he draws, the tape is stopped and a few lines from *The Resisting Reader* are spoken by a female performer, ending with the phrase "the demonstration of how to murder your wife and get away with it." During this phrase, the male performer's drawing becomes agitated and he covers the woman's face and body with red scribbling; a blackout follows.

I am evolving my own feminist means of directing. *Resisting the Birth Mark* was developed in a collaborative process with students at Georgia State University and performed in January 1990. In the course of rehearsals the mass murder of fourteen women engineering students in Montreal caused a strong reaction among the cast and I interpolated a scene into the piece in which the male performer says, "You're all a bunch of feminists. I hate feminists," one woman says, "I'm not a feminist," and the male performer mimes mowing down all the women with a machine gun. The slumping down of the stage manager is followed by a blackout.

I plan to continue writing other theory plays, creating a full evening of one-acts, using anthropological field work, psychological case histories, and other forms of male-written texts in combination with relevant feminist theories. The amount of feminist text will vary from play to play, but the structures will embody feminist ideas in all cases. This is feminist theory in action for me. I hope that the future will find many in theater performing all kinds of acts and theories that will bring to the stage, as well as to the critical page, the passion of attention to women.

Notes

Chapter 1

1. Sue-Ellen Case, *Feminism and Theatre* (New York: Methuen, 1988); and Jill Dolan, *The Feminist Spectator as Critic* (Ann Arbor, Mich.: UMI Research Press, 1988). Subsequent page numbers in parentheses.

2. Alison M. Jagger, *Feminist Politics and Human Nature* (Totowa, N.J.: Rowman and Allanheld, 1983).

3. See, for instance, Alice Echols, "The New Feminism of Yin and Yang," in *Powers of Desire: The Politics of Sexuality,* ed. Ann Snitow et al. (New York: Monthly Review Press, 1983); Linda Alcoff, "Cultural Feminism versus Post-Structuralism: The Identity Crisis in Feminist Theory," *Signs* 13 (Spring 1988): 405–36; and Teresa de Lauretis, "The Essence of the Triangle; or, Taking the Risk of Essentialism Seriously: Feminist Theory in Italy, the U.S., and Britian," *differences* 1 (Summer 1989): 3–37, and other articles in that issue.

4. For further examples of materialist theory and practice, see essays by Catherine Belsey and Michèle Barrett in Judith Newton and Deborah Rosenfelt, eds., *Feminist Criticism and Social Change: Sex, Class, and Race in Literature and Culture* (New York: Methuen, 1985), Yvonne Yarbro-Bejarano, "The Female Subject in Chicano Theatre: Sexuality, 'Race,' and Class," *Theatre Journal* 38 (December 1986): 389–407; and some of the essays in Lynda Hart, ed., *Making a Spectacle: Feminist Essays on Contemporary Women's Theatre* (Ann Arbor: University of Michigan Press, 1989).

5. Case, *Feminism and Theatre,* 95.

6. Barbara Smith, "Toward a Black Feminist Criticism," in *The New Feminist Criticism,* ed. Elaine Showalter (New York: Pantheon, 1985), 172. Subsequent page numbers in parentheses.

7. Deborah E. McDowell, "New Directions for Black Feminist Criticism," in *The New Feminist Criticism,* ed. Elaine Showalter (New York: Pantheon, 1985), 191. Subsequent page numbers in parentheses.

8. For example, see Barbara Christian, *Black Feminist Criticism: Perspectives on Black Women Writers* (New York: Pergamon Press, 1985); Susan Willis, "Black Women Writers: Taking A Critical Perspective," in *Making a Difference,* ed. Gayle Greene and Coppélia Kahn (New York: Methuen, 1985); and two review essays by Claudia Tate, "On Black Literary Women and the Evolution of Critical Discourse" and "Reshuffling the Deck; or, (Re)Reading Race and Gender in Black Women's Writing," *Tulsa Studies in Women's Literature* 5 (Spring 1986): 111–23, and 7 (Spring 1988): 119–32. Also, see Maggie Humm, *Feminist Criticism: Women as Contemporary Critics* (New York: St. Martin's Press, 1986), chap. 6, for a discussion of the relationship of black and lesbian criticism and an overview of those fields (1970–85).

9. Valerie Smith, "Gender and Afro-Americanist Literary Theory and Criticism," in *Speaking of Gender,* ed. Elaine Showalter (New York: Routledge, 1989), 62.

10. See, among others, Jeanne-Marie A. Miller, "Black Women Playwrights from Grimke to Shange: Selected Synopses of Their Works," in *But Some of Us Are Brave: Black Women's Studies,* ed. Gloria T. Hull et al. (Old Westbury, N.Y.: Feminist Press, 1982); Margaret B. Wilkerson, ed. *9 Plays by Black Women* (New York: New American Library, 1986); Margaret B. Wilkerson, *"A Raisin in the Sun:* Anniversary of an American Classic," *Theatre Journal* 38 (December 1986): 441–52, and "Music as Metaphor: New Plays of Black Women," in *Making a Spectacle,* ed. Lynda Hart (Ann Arbor: University of Michigan Press, 1989); Elizabeth Brown-Guillory, *Their Place on Stage: Black Women Playwrights in America* (Westport, Conn.: Greenwood Press, 1988); Glenda Dickerson, "The Cult of True Womanhood: Toward a Womanist Attitude in African-American Theatre," *Theatre Journal* 40 (May 1988): 178–87; and Kathy A. Perkins, *Black Female Playwrights: Plays before 1950* (Bloomington: Indiana University Press, 1989).

11. bell hooks, *Feminist Theory: From Margin to Center* (Boston: South End Press, 1984); Deborah K. King, "Multiple Jeopardy, Multiple Consciousness: The Context of a Black Feminist Ideology," *Signs* 14 (Autumn 1988): 42–72; and Patricia Hill Collins, "The Social

Construction of Black Feminist Thought," *Signs* 14 (Summer 1989): 745–73.

12. Barbara Christian, "The Race for Theory," *Feminist Studies* 14 (Spring 1988): 68. Subsequent page numbers in parentheses.

13. Jane Marcus, "Storming the Toolshed," in *Feminist Theory*, ed. Nannerl O. Keohane et al. (Chicago: University of Chicago Press, 1982), 217–35.

14. Nina Baym, "The Madwoman and Her Languages: Why I Don't Do Feminist Literary Theory," and Laurie Finke, "The Rhetoric of Marginality: Why I Do Feminist Theory," *Tulsa Studies in Women's Literature* 3 (Spring–Fall 1984): 45, and 5 (Fall 1986): 251–72.

15. Elizabeth A. Meese, *Crossing the Double-Cross: The Practice of Feminist Criticism* (Chapel Hill: University of North Carolina Press, 1986), 144, 150.

16. Ruth Salvaggio, "Theory and Space, Space and Women," *Tulsa Studies in Women's Literature* 7 (Fall 1988): 273.

17. Jill Dolan, "In Defense of the Discourse: Materialist Feminism, Postmodernism, Poststructuralism . . . and Theory," *TDR* 33 (Fall 1989): 64–65.

18. Bonnie Zimmerman, "What Has Never Been: An Overview of Lesbian Feminist Criticism," in *Making a Difference*, ed. Gayle Greene and Coppélia Kahn (New York: Methuen, 1985), 178–79. Subsequent page numbers in parentheses.

19. Adrienne Rich, "Compulsory Heterosexuality and Lesbian Existence," *Signs* 5 (Summer 1980): 632. Subsequent page numbers in parentheses.

20. Ann Ferguson et al., "On 'Compulsory Heterosexuality and Lesbian Existence': Defining the Issues," in *Feminist Theory*, ed. Nannerl O. Keohane et al. (Chicago: University of Chicago Press, 1982), 148–49.

21. Ibid., 167, 172.

22. Monique Wittig, "One is Not Born A Woman," *Feminist Issues* 1 (Winter 1981): 47–54, and "The Point of View: Universal or Particular?" *Feminist Issues* 3 (Fall 1983): 63–69, among others.

23. Marilyn R. Farwell, "Toward a Definition of the Lesbian Literary Imagination," *Signs* 14 (Autumn 1988): 100–118.

24. Kaier Curtin, *"We Can Always Call Them Bulgarians": The Emergence of Lesbians and Gay Men on the American Stage* (Boston: Alyson Publications, 1987).

25. Rosemary K. Curb, "Re/cognition, Re/presentation, Re/creation in Woman-Conscious Drama: The Seer, the Seen, the Scene, the Obscene," *Theatre Journal* 37 (October 1985): 302–16.

26. Jill Dolan, "The Dynamics of Desire: Sexuality and Gender in Pornography and Performance," *Theatre Journal* 39 (May 1987): 156–74; "Desire Cloaked in a Trenchcoat," *TDR* 33 (Spring 1989): 59–67; "Breaking the Code: Musings on Lesbian Sexuality and the Performer," *Modern Drama* 32 (March 1989): 146–58; "Feminists, Lesbians, and Other Women in Theatre: Thoughts on the Politics of Performance," in *Women in Theatre,* Themes in Drama Series, no. 11 (New York: Cambridge University Press, 1989); and "'Lesbian' Subjectivity in Realism: Dragging at the Margins of Structure and Ideology," in *Performing Feminisms,* ed. Sue-Ellen Case (Baltimore: Johns Hopkins University Press, 1990).

27. Dolan, *The Feminist Spectator as Critic,* 63.

28. Kate Davy, "Constructing the Spectator: Reception, Context, and Address in Lesbian Performance," *Performing Arts Journal* 10 (Fall 1986): 43–52, and "Reading Past the Heterosexual Imperative: *Dress Suits to Hire,*" *TDR* 33 (Spring 1989): 157–70; Teresa de Lauretis: "Sexual Indifference and Lesbian Representation," *Theatre Journal* 40 (May 1988): 155–77; Sue-Ellen Case, "Judy Grahn's Gynopoetics: *The Queen of Swords,*" *Studies in the Literary Imagination* 21 (Fall 1988) 47–67, and "Toward a Butch-Femme Aesthetic," in *Making a Spectacle,* ed. Lynda Hart (Ann Arbor: University of Michigan Press, 1989).

29. Gerda Lerner, *The Majority Finds Its Past: Placing Women in History* (New York: Oxford University Press, 1979), 149. Subsequent page numbers in parentheses. For a feminist perspective on the historiography of theater, see Tracy C. Davis, "Questions for a Feminist Methodology in Theatre History," in *Interpreting the Theatrical Past,* ed. Thomas Postlewait and Bruce A. McConachie (Iowa City: University of Iowa Press, 1989).

30. Joan Kelly, *Women, History and Theory: The Essays of Joan Kelly* (Chicago: University of Chicago Press, 1984), 19.

31. Elizabeth Abel, "Introduction," in *Writing and Sexual Difference,* ed. Abel (Chicago: University of Chicago Press, 1982), 1–2.

32. Elaine Showalter, ed., *The New Feminist Criticism: Essays on Women, Literature, and Theory* (New York: Pantheon, 1985), 8–9.

33. Janelle Reinelt, "Feminist Theory and the Problem of Performance," *Modern Drama* 32 (March 1989): 48–51.

34. Lynda Hart, "Introduction: Performing Feminism," in *Making a Spectacle,* ed. Hart (Ann Arbor: University of Michigan Press, 1989), 3.

35. Kate Millett, *Sexual Politics* (New York: Doubleday, 1970); Marjorie Rosen, *Popcorn Venus* (New York: Avon, 1973); and Molly Haskell,

From Reverence to Rape: The Treatment of Women in the Movies (Middlesex, Eng.: Penguin, 1974).

36. Carolyn R. Lenz et al., *The Woman's Part: Feminist Criticism of Shakespeare* (Urbana: University of Illinois Press, 1980); Linda Bamber, *Comic Women, Tragic Men: A Study of Gender and Genre in Shakespeare* (Palo Alto, Calif.: Stanford University Press, 1981); Irene G. Dash, *Wooing, Wedding, and Power: Women in Shakespeare's Plays* (New York: Columbia University Press, 1981); and Marilyn French, *Shakespeare's Division of Experience* (New York: Ballantine, 1981).

37. Marianne L. Novy, *Love's Argument: Gender Relations in Shakespeare* (Chapel Hill: University of North Carolina Press, 1984); Phyllis Rackin, "Anti-Historians: Women's Roles in Shakespeare's Histories," *Theatre Journal* 37 (October 1985): 329–44, and "Androgyny, Mimesis, and the Marriage of the Boy Heroine on the English Renaissance Stage," in *Speaking of Gender,* ed. Elaine Showalter (New York: Routledge, 1989); Lorraine Helms, "Playing the Woman's Part: Feminist Criticism and Shakespearean Performance," *Theatre Journal* 41 (May 1989): 190–200; Kathleen McLuskie, *Renaissance Dramatists,* and Dympna Callaghan, *Woman and Gender in Renaissance Tragedy* (both from Atlantic Highlands, N.J.: Humanities Press International, 1989); Carol Rutter, *Clamorous Voices: Shakespeare's Women Today* (New York: Routledge, 1989); Marianne Novy, ed., *Women's Re-Visions of Shakespeare* (Champaign: University of Illinois Press, 1990); and Katherine E. Kelly, "The Queen's Two Bodies: Shakespeare's Boy Actress in Breeches," *Theatre Journal* 42 (March 1990): 81–93.

38. Catherine Clément, *Opera; or, the Undoing of Women,* trans. Betsy Wing (Minneapolis: University of Minnesota Press, 1988); Gail Finney, *Women in Modern Drama: Freud, Feminism, and European Theater at the Turn of the Century* (Ithaca, N.Y.: Cornell University Press, 1989); Michelene Wandor, *Look Back in Gender: Sexuality and the Family in Post-War British Drama* (New York: Methuen, 1987); June Schlueter, ed. *Feminist Rereadings of Modern American Drama* (Madison, N.J.: Fairleigh Dickinson University Press, 1989), Lesley Ferris, *Acting Women: Images of Women in Theater* (New York: New York University Press, 1989); and *Women in Theatre,* Themes in Drama Series, no. 11 (New York: Cambridge University Press, 1989), which also contains some second-stage work on women playwrights.

39. Among others, Victoria Sullivan and James Hatch, eds., *Plays by and about Women* (New York: Random House, 1973); Honor Moore, ed., *The New Women's Theatre* (New York: Random House, 1977);

Rachel France, ed., *A Century of Plays by American Women* (New York: Richard Rosen Press, 1979); and Judith E. Barlow, ed., *Plays by American Women: The Early Years* (New York: Avon, 1981; later reissued by Applause Books).

40. Janet Brown, *Feminist Drama: Definition and Critical Analysis* (Metuchen, N.J.: Scarecrow Press, 1979); Dinah Leavitt, *Feminist Theatre Groups* (Jefferson, N.C.: McFarland and Co., 1980); and Elizabeth J. Natalle, *Feminist Theatre: A Study in Persuasion* (Metuchen, N.J.: Scarecrow Press, 1985).

41. Brenda Coven, *American Women Dramatists of the Twentieth Century: A Bibliography* (Metuchen, N.J.: Scarecrow Press, 1982). Some bibliographies also appeared within other books, such as the one edited by Chinoy and Jenkins.

42. Among the books, Nancy Cotton, *Women Playwrights in England c. 1363–1750* (Lewisburg, Pa.: Bucknell University Press, 1980); Judith Olauson, *The American Woman Playwright: A View of Criticism and Characterization* (Troy, N.Y.: Whitston, 1981); Helen Krich Chinoy and Linda Walsh Jenkins, *Women in American Theatre: Careers, Images, Movements* (New York: Crown, 1981; rev. ed., New York: Theatre Communications Group, 1987); Karen Malpede, ed., *Women in Theatre: Compassion and Hope* (New York: Drama Book Publishers, 1983); Helene Keyssar, *Feminist Theatre: An Introduction to Plays of Contemporary British and American Women* (New York: Grove, 1985); Kathleen Betsko and Rachel Koenig, *Interviews with Contemporary Women Playwrights* (New York: Beech Tree Books, 1987); and *Studies in American Drama, 1945–Present* 4 ("American Women Playwrights" issue, 1989).

43. Among many others, Janelle Reinelt, "Beyond Brecht: Britain's New Feminist Drama," *Theatre Journal* 38 (May 1986): 154–63; Susan Carlson, "Process and Product: Contemporary British Theatre and Its Communities of Women," *Theatre Research International* 13 (Autumn 1988): 249–63, and "Self and Sexuality: Contemporary British Women Playwrights and the Problem of Sexual Identity," *Journal of Dramatic Theory and Criticism* 3 (Spring 1989): 157–78; Loren Kruger, "The Display's the Thing: Gender and Public Sphere in Comtemporary British Theater," *Theatre Journal* 42 (March 1990): 27–47; Jane Moss, "Women's Theater in France," *Signs* 12 (Spring 1987): 548–67; Judith Graves Miller, "Contemporary Women's Voices in French Theatre," *Modern Drama* 32 (March 1989): 5–23, and other articles in that issue; Teresa L. Jillson, "Working Women's Words and the Conditions of Their Production(s)," *Journal of Dramatic Theory and Criticism* 2 (Spring 1988):

135–48; Sue-Ellen Case and Ellen Donkin, "FIT: Germany's First Conference for Women in Theatre," *Women & Performance* 2 (1985): 65–73; Ralph Ley, "Beyond 1984: Provocation and Prognosis in Marieluise Fleisser's Play *Purgatory in Ingolstadt*," *Modern Drama* 31 (September 1988): 340–51. Yvonne Yarbro-Bejarano, "Chicanas' Experience in Collective Theater: Ideology and Form," *Women & Performance* 2 (1985): 45–58; Sandra Messinger Cypess, "From Colonial Constructs to Feminist Figures: Re/visions by Mexican Women Dramatists," *Theatre Journal* 41 (December 1989): 492–504; and Patricia W. O'Connor, "Women Playwrights in Contemporary Spain and the Male-Dominated Canon," *Signs* 15 (Winter 1990): 376–90.

44. Lynda Hart, ed., *Making A Spectacle: Feminist Essays on Contemporary Women's Theatre* (Ann Arbor: University of Michigan Press, 1989); and Enoch Brater, ed., *Feminine Focus: The New Women Playwrights* (New York: Oxford Unversity Press, 1989).

45. Elin Diamond, "Brechtian Theory / Feminist Theory: Toward a Gestic Feminist Criticism," *TDR* 32 (Spring 1988): 82–94, and *Theatre Journal* 40 ("Feminist Diversions" issue, May 1988).

46. See for example, Jeannette Laillou Savona and Ann Wilson, "Introduction," *Modern Drama* 32 ("Women in the Theatre" issue, March 1989): 1–4; Jeanie Forte, "Realism, Narrative, and the Feminist Playwright—A Problem of Reception," and Elin Diamond, "Mimesis, Mimicry, and the 'True-Real,'" both also in *Modern Drama* 32; and Diamond's book *Feminist Stagings: Unmaking Mimesis* (New York: Routledge, forthcoming).

47. Linda Walsh Jenkins, "Locating the Language of Gender Experience," *Women & Performance* 2 (1984): 5–20;.Josette Féral, "Writing and Displacement: Women in Theatre," *Modern Drama* 27 (December 1984): 549–63; Rosemary K. Curb, "Re/cognition, Re/presentation, Re/creation in Woman-Conscious Drama: The Seer, the Seen, the Scene, the Obscene," *Theatre Journal* 37 (October 1985): 302–16; Jeanie Forte, "Women's Performance Art: Feminism and Postmodernism," *Theatre Journal* 40 (May 1988): 217–35.

48. Sue-Ellen Case, ed., *Performing Feminisims: Feminist Critical Theory and Theatre* (Baltimore: Johns Hopkins University Press, 1990); and Susan M. Flierl Steadman, "Feminist Dramatic Criticism: Where We Are Now," *Women & Performance* 4 (1989): 118–48.

49. Jill Dolan, "Gender Impersonation Onstage: Destroying or Maintaining the Mirror of Gender Roles?" *Women & Performance* 2 (1985): 7, 10.

50. Case, *Feminism and Theatre*, 131–32.

Chapter 2

1. Elaine Showalter, "Review Essay: Literary Criticism," *Signs* 1 (Winter 1975): 435–60; Annette Kolodny, "Review Essay: Literary Criticism," *Signs* 2 (Winter 1976): 404–21; Sydney Janet Kaplan, "Review Essay: Literary Criticism," *Signs* 4 (Spring 1979): 514–27; Cheri Register, "Review Essay: Literary Criticism," *Signs* 6 (Winter 1980): 268–82; and Betsy Draine, "Refusing the Wisdom of Solomon: Some Recent Feminist Literary Theory," *Signs* 15 (Autumn 1989): 144–70.

2. Kolodny, "Review Essay," 420.

3. Kaplan, "Review Essay," 527.

4. Register, "Review Essay," 274, 281.

5. Cheri Register, "American Feminist Literary Criticism: A Bibliographical Introduction," in *Feminist Literary Criticism,* ed. Josephine Donovan (Lexington: University of Kentucky Press, 1975), 2, 19.

6. Elaine Showalter, "Women's Time, Women's Space: Writing the History of Feminist Criticism," *Tulsa Studies in Women's Literature* 3 (Spring–Fall 1984): 36.

7. Sydney Janet Kaplan, "Varieties of Feminist Criticism," in *Making a Difference,* ed. Gayle Greene and Coppélia Kahn (New York: Methuen, 1985), 37–58.

8. Toril Moi, *Sexual/Textual Politics: Feminist Literary Theory* (New York: Methuen, 1985); and Janet Todd, *Feminist Literary History* (New York: Routledge, 1988).

9. Draine, "Refusing the Wisdom of Solomon," 170.

10. Susan Koppelman Cornillon, ed., *Images of Women in Fiction: Feminist Perspectives* (Bowling Green, Ohio: Bowling Green University Press, 1972); Josephine Donovan, ed. *Feminist Literary Criticism: Explorations in Theory* (Lexington: University of Kentucky Press, 1975); Arlyn Diamond and Lee R. Edwards, eds., *The Authority of Experience: Essays in Feminist Criticism* (Boston: University of Massachusetts Press, 1977); Cheryl L. Brown and Karen Olson, eds., *Feminist Criticism: Essays on Theory, Poetry and Prose* (Metuchen, N.J.: Scarecrow Press, 1978); Mary Jacobus, ed., *Women Writing and Writing about Women* (New York: Harper and Row, 1979).

11. Elaine Showalter, "Towards A Feminist Poetics" (1979) and "Feminist Criticism in the Wilderness" (1981), and Annette Kolodny, "A Map for Rereading: Gender and the Interpretation of Literary Texts" (1980) and "Dancing Through the Minefield: Some Observations on the Theory, Practice, and Politics of a Feminist Literary Criticism" (1980);

all four in *The New Feminist Criticism,* ed. Showalter (New York: Pantheon, 1985).

12. Compare Showalter's "Introduction: The Rise of Gender," in *Speaking of Gender* (New York: Routledge, 1989), 1–13, with Kolodny's "Dancing Between Left and Right: Feminism and the Academic Minefield in the 1980s," *Feminist Studies* 14 (Fall 1988): 453–66.

13. Elizabeth Abel, ed., *Writing and Sexual Difference* (Chicago: University of Chicago Press, 1982); Elaine Showalter, ed., *The New Feminist Criticism: Essays on Women, Literature, and Theory* (New York: Pantheon, 1985); Gayle Green and Coppélia Kahn, eds., *Making a Difference: Feminist Literary Criticism* (New York: Methuen, 1985); Nancy K. Miller, ed., *The Poetics of Gender,* Gender and Culture Series (New York: Columbia University Press, 1986); Mary Eagleton, ed., *Feminist Literary Theory: A Reader* (Oxford, Eng., and New York: Basil Blackwell, 1986); and Elaine Showalter, ed., *Speaking of Gender* (New York: Routledge, 1989).

14. Catherine Rainwater and William J. Scheick, eds., *Contemporary American Women Writers: Narrative Strategies* (Lexington: University Press of Kentucky, 1985); and Rachel Blau DuPlessis, *Writing beyond the Ending: Narrative Strategies of Twentieth-Century Women Writers* (Bloomington: Indiana University Press, 1985).

15. Teresa de Lauretis, ed., *Feminist Studies / Critical Studies,* Theories of Contemporary Culture Series, vol. 8 (Bloomington: Indiana University Press, 1986); and Susan Sheridan, ed., *Grafts: Feminist Cultural Criticism* (New York: Verso, 1988).

16. Christine Froula, "When Eve Reads Milton: Undoing the Canonical Economy," *Critical Inquiry* 10 (December 1983): 321–47; Edward Pechter, "Critical Response I: When Pechter Reads Froula Pretending She's Eve Reading Milton; or, New Feminist Is But Old Priest Writ Large," *Critical Inquiry* 11 (September 1984): 163–70; Christine Froula, "Critical Response II: Pechter's Specter: Milton's Bogey Writ Small; or, Why Is He Afraid of Virginia Woolf?" *Critical Inquiry* 11 (September 1984): 171–78.

17. Gayatri Chakravorty Spivak, translator's preface to Jacques Derrida, *Of Grammatology* (Baltimore: Johns Hopkins University Press, 1976); "Displacement and the Discourse of Woman," in *Displacement: Derrida and After,* ed. Mark Krupnick (Bloomington: Indiana University Press, 1983); and "Feminism and Critical Theory," in *For Alma Mater: Theory and Practice in Feminist Scholarship,* ed. Paula Treichler et al. (Champaign: University of Illinois Press, 1985).

18. For example, Elizabeth A. Meese, *Crossing the Double-Cross: The*

Practice of Feminist Criticism (Chapel Hill: University of North Carolina Press, 1986).

19. For an introduction to the field, see Jane P. Tompkins, ed., *Reader-Response Criticism: From Formalism to Post-Structuralism* (Baltimore: Johns Hopkins University Press, 1980); Susan Suleiman and Inge Crosman, eds., *The Reader in the Text: Essays on Audience and Interpretation* (Princeton University Press, 1980); and later, feminist applications in Elizabeth A. Flynn and Patrocinio P. Schweickart, eds., *Gender and Reading: Essays on Readers, Texts, and Contexts* (Baltimore: Johns Hopkins University Press, 1986).

20. Judith Fetterley, *The Resisting Reader: A Feminist Approach to American Fiction* (Bloomington: Indiana University Press, 1978). Subsequent page numbers in parentheses.

21. See Case, *Feminism and Theatre*, 6; Dolan, *The Feminist Spectator as Critic*, 2; and Finney, *Women in Modern Drama*, 20.

22. Among recent articles are Judith Fetterley, "Reading about Reading," in *Gender and Reading*, ed. Elizabeth A. Flynn and Patrocinio P. Schweickart (Baltimore: Johns Hopkins University Press, 1986), 147–54; C. W. E. Bigsby, "Introduction," in *Plays by Susan Glaspell*, ed. Bigsby (Cambridge: Cambridge University Press, 1987), 1–31; J. Ellen Gainor, "A Stage of Her Own: Susan Glaspell's *The Verge* and Women's Dramaturgy," *Journal of American Drama and Theatre* 1 (Spring 1989): 79–99; and Linda Ben-Zvi, "Susan Glaspell's Contributions to Contemporary Women Playwrights," in *Feminine Focus*, ed. Enoch Brater (New York: Oxford University Press, 1989).

23. Eugene O'Neill, *The Iceman Cometh* (New York: Random House, 1940; reprint ed., New York: Vintage Books, 1957), v. Subsequent page numbers in parentheses.

Chapter 3

1. Victor Turner, "Frame, Flow, and Reflection: Ritual and Drama as Public Liminality," in *Performance in Postmodern Culture,* ed. Michel Benamou and Charles Caramello (Madison, Wis.: Coda Press, 1977), 33. For more discussion of liminality, see Turner's *The Anthropology of Performance* and *From Ritual to Theatre.*

2. Victor Turner, *From Ritual to Theatre: The Human Seriousness of Play* (New York: Performing Arts Journal Publications, 1982).

3. Michelle Z. Rosaldo and Louise Lamphere, eds., *Women, Culture, and Society* (Stanford, Calif.: Stanford University Press, 1974), 13.

4. Rayna R. Reiter, ed., *Toward an Anthropology of Women* (New York: Monthly Review Press, 1975), 19.

5. Sally McConnell-Ginet et al., eds. *Women and Language in Literature and Society* (New York: Praeger, 1980).

6. Sherry B. Ortner and Harriet Whitehead, eds., *Sexual Meanings* (Cambridge: Cambridge University Press, 1981), 7.

7. Jane Monnig Atkinson, "Review Essay: Anthropology," *Signs* 8 (Winter 1982): 238. Subsequent page numbers in parentheses.

8. Marilyn Strathern, "An Awkward Relationship: The Case of Feminism and Anthropology," *Signs* 12 (Winter 1987): 277.

9. Henrietta L. Moore, *Feminism and Anthropology*, (Minneapolis: University of Minnesota Press, 1988). Subsequent page numbers in parentheses.

10. In Reiter, *Toward an Anthropology of Women*, 157–210. Subsequent page numbers in parentheses.

11. Diamond, "Refusing the Romanticism of Identity," 275; Case, "Classic Drag," 319; and Rackin, "Anti-Historians," 337.

12. Nancy Hartsock, *Money, Sex, and Power: Toward a Feminist Historical Materialism* (New York: Longman, 1983), 295.

13. Eve Kosofsky Sedgwick, *Between Men* (New York: Columbia University Press, 1985).

14. Eve Kosofsky Sedgwick, "Sexualism and the Citizen of the World: Wycherley, Stern, and Male Homosocial Desire," *Critical Inquiry* 11 (December 1984): 227.

15. Ibid., 228–29.

16. Sedgwick, *Between Men*, 25–26.

17. Ibid., 21.

18. Arthur Miller, *Death of a Salesman* (New York: Viking, 1949), 90. Subsequent page numbers in parentheses.

19. Mary L. Broe, "Bohemia Bumps into Calvin: The Deception of Passivity in Lillian Hellman's Drama," *Southern Quarterly* 19 (Winter 1981): 26–41.

20. Lillian Hellman, *Another Part of the Forest*, in *The Collected Plays* (Boston: Little, Brown, 1972), 382. Subsequent page numbers in parentheses.

21. Rubin, "The Traffic in Women," 196.

Chapter 4

1. Mary Brown Parlee, "Review Essay: Psychology and Women," *Signs* 5 (Autumn 1979): 123–28.

2. Mary Brown Parlee, "Psychology of Women in the Eighties: Promising Problems," *International Journal of Women's Studies* 8 (March–April 1985): 200.

3. Shirley Nelson Garner, Claire Kahane, and Madelon Sprengnether, eds., *The (M)other Tongue: Essays in Feminist Psychoanalytic Interpretation* (Ithaca, N.Y.: Cornell University Press, 1985), 20.

4. Ann Rosalind Jones, "Inscribing Femininity: French Theories of the Feminine," in *Making a Difference,* ed. Gayle Greene and Coppélia Kahn, 80. Subsequent page numbers in parentheses.

5. Elaine Marks and Isabelle de Courtivron, eds., *New French Feminisms* (Amherst, Mass.: University of Massachusetts Press, 1980; reprint ed., New York: Schocken Books, 1981); *Feminist Studies* 7 (Summer 1981); *Yale French Studies* 62 (1981); *Signs* 7 (Fall 1981); *Critical Inquiry* 8 (Winter 1981). See also *Paragraph* 8 (October 1986).

6. For example, Irigaray's *Speculum of the Other Woman* and *This Sex Which Is Not One* (1985); *The Newly Born Woman,* by Cixous and Clément (1986); *Desire in Language* (1980), *Revolution in Poetic Language* (1984), and *The Kristeva Reader* (1986), all by Kristeva; and several essays in *Feminist Issues* by Wittig.

7. Nancy K. Miller, ed., *The Poetics of Gender,* Gender and Culture Series (New York: Columbia University Press, 1986), has essays by Wittig, Alice Jardine, Jane Gallop, and Domna C. Stanton. See also Toril Moi, *Sexual/Textual Politics: Feminist Literary Theory* (New York: Methuen, 1985), for summaries of the major theorists, and *French Feminist Thought: A Reader* (New York: Basil Blackwell, 1987), for writings by other French feminists; books by Jane Gallop, including *The Daughter's Seduction: Feminism and Psychoanalysis* (Ithaca, N.Y.: Cornell University Press, 1982) and *Thinking through the Body* (New York: Columbia University Press, 1988); and Rosemarie Tong's *Feminist Thought: A Comprehensive Introduction* (Boulder, Colo.: Westview Press, 1989) for summaries of both psychoanalytic feminism and French feminists.

8. In *Benmussa Directs* (London: John Calder, 1979) and in *Diacritics* 13 (Spring 1983): 2–32.

9. Ann Wilson, "History and Hysteria: Writing the Body in *Portrait of Dora* and *Signs of Life,*" *Modern Drama* 32 (March 1989): 73–88.

10. Elin Diamond, "Mimesis, Mimicry, and the 'True Real,'" *Modern Drama* 32 (March 1989): 58–72. See also Diamond's *Feminist Stagings: Unmaking Mimesis* (New York: Routledge, forthcoming).

11. Surveys of this work are in two anthologies: Richard Feldstein and Judith Roof, eds., *Feminism and Psychoanalysis* (Ithaca, N.Y.: Cornell

University Press, 1989); and Teresa Brennan, ed., *Between Feminism and Psychoanalysis* (New York: Routledge, 1989).

12. Mary Roth Walsh, ed., *The Psychology of Women: Ongoing Debates* (New Haven: Yale University Press, 1987).

13. Jean Shinoda Bolen, *Goddesses in Everywoman: A New Psychology of Women* (New York: Harper and Row, 1984).

14. *Women & Therapy: A Feminist Quarterly* 6 ("Race and Gender" issue, Winter 1987).

15. Judith Kegan Gardiner, "Mind Mother: Psychoanalysis and Feminism," in *Making a Difference,* ed. Gayle Greene and Coppélia Kahn, 130.

16. Adrienne Rich, *Of Woman Born: Motherhood as Experience and Institution* (New York: Norton, 1976); Dorothy Dinnerstein, *The Mermaid and the Minotaur: Sexual Arrangements and Human Malaise* (New York: Harper and Row, 1976); Nancy Chodorow, *The Reproduction of Mothering: Psychoanalysois and the Sociology of Gender* (Berkeley: University of California Press, 1978).

17. Coppélia Kahn, "The Hand That Rocks the Cradle: Recent Gender Theories And Their Implications," in *The (M)other Tongue,* ed. Garner et al., 73.

18. Gardiner, "Mind Mother," 133–34.

19. Jane Flax, "The Conflict between Nurturance and Autonomy in Mother-Daughter Relationships and within Feminism," *Feminist Studies* 4 (June 1978): 171–89.

20. Jessica Benjamin, "A Desire of One's Own: Psychoanalytic Feminism and Intersubjective Space," in *Feminist Studies / Critical Studies,* ed. Teresa de Lauretis (Bloomington: Indiana University Press, 1986), 83, 97–98.

21. Marianne Hirsch, "Review Essay: Mothers and Daughters," *Signs* 7 (Autumn 1981): 205.

22. Ibid., 221. Eight years later Hirsch published the result of following her own advice: *The Mother/Daughter Plot: Narrative, Psychoanalysis, Feminism* (Bloomington: Indiana University Press, 1989).

23. Nancy Chodorow, "Being and Doing: A Cross-Cultural Examination of the Socialization of Males and Females," in *Woman in Sexist Society: Studies in Power and Powerlessness,* ed. Vivian Gornick and Barbara K. Moran (New York: Basic Books, 1971; reprint ed., New York: New American Library, 1972), 287. This and the next two essays mentioned appear in a collection of Chodorow's essays, *Feminism and Psychoanalytic Theory* (New Haven: Yale University Press, 1989), which also includes essays written after *Reproduction* and an introduction that includes Chodorow's views of her earlier work from the vantage point of 1989.

24. Nancy Chodorow, "Family Structure and Feminine Personality," in *Women, Culture, and Society,* ed. Rosaldo and Lampere, 43.

25. Ibid., 52.

26. Nancy Chodorow, "Oedipal Asymmetries and Heterosexual Knots," *Social Problems* 23 (1976): 454–68.

27. Nancy Chodorow, "Mothering, Object-Relations, and the Female Oedipal Configuration," *Feminist Studies* 4 (February 1978): 137.

28. Ibid., 150.

29. Ibid., 151.

30. Kahn, "The Hand That Rocks the Cradle," 76.

31. Judith Lorber et al., "On *The Reproduction of Mothering:* A Methodological Debate," *Signs* 6 (Spring 1981): 482–514; Adrienne Rich, "Compulsory Heterosexuality and Lesbian Existence," *Signs* 5 (Summer 1980): 631–60; Elizabeth V. Spelman, *Inessential Woman: Problems of Exclusion in Feminist Thought* (Boston: Beacon Press, 1989), 80–113; and Nancy Fraser and Linda J. Nicholson, "Social Criticism without Philosophy: An Encounter between Feminism and Postmodernism," in *Feminism/Postmodernism,* ed. Nicholson (New York: Routledge, 1990), 29–31.

32. Chodorow, *The Reproduction of Mothering,* 109. Subsequent page numbers in parentheses.

33. Laurie Stone, "Mother Lode," *Village Voice,* 25 April 1989, 96.

34. Jenny S. Spencer, "Norman's *'night, Mother:* Psycho-Drama of Female Identity," *Modern Drama* 30 (September 1987): 370.

35. Millicent Dillon, *A Little Original Sin: The Life and Work of Jane Bowles* (New York: Holt, Rinehart, 1981), 95. Subsequent page numbers in parentheses.

36. Bowles worked on the play in New York between 1945 and 1947 and published the first act in 1947. The play was produced first at the Hedgerow Theater in Pennsylvania in 1951 and next at the University of Michigan in 1953 (Dillon, *A Little Original Sin,* 121, 132, 219, 226).

37. *My Sister's Hand In Mine: An Expanded Edition of the Collected Works of Jane Bowles* (New York: Ecco Press, 1978), 208. Subsequent page numbers in parentheses.

38. Chodorow, *Reproduction of Mothering,* 138.

39. Sue-Ellen Case, "Re-Viewing Hrotsvit," *Theatre Journal* 35 (December 1983): 534.

Chapter 5

1. Case, *Feminism and Theatre,* 115. Subsequent page numbers in parentheses.

2. See Keir Elam, *The Semiotics of Theatre and Drama* (New York: Methuen, 1980); Patrice Pavis, *Languages of the Stage: Essays in the Semiology of the Theatre* (New York: Performing Arts Journal Publications, 1982); Martin Esslin, *The Field of Drama: How the Signs of Drama Create Meaning on Stage and Screen* (New York: Methuen, 1987); and Marvin Carlson, *Places of Performance: The Semiotics of Theatre Architecture* (Ithaca, N.Y.: Cornell University Press, 1989), and *Theatre Semiotics: Signs of Life* (Bloomington: Indiana University Press, 1990), among others.

3. Sue-Ellen Case, "From Split Subject to Split Britches," in *Feminine Focus*, ed. Enoch Brater (New York: Oxford University Press, 1989), 129.

4. Kaja Silverman, *The Subject of Semiotics* (New York: Oxford University Press, 1983), 130. Subsequent page numbers in parentheses.

5. Janey Place and Julianne Burton, "Feminist Film Criticism," *Movie*, no.22 (Spring 1976): 62.

6. Christine Gledhill, "Recent Developments in Feminist Criticism," *Quarterly Review of Film Studies* 3 (Fall 1978): 479.

7. Ibid., 491. For an additional view, see Laura E. Donaldson, "(ex)Changing (wo)Man: Towards a Materialist-Feminist Semiotics," *Cultural Critique*, no. 11 (Winter 1988–89): 5–23

8. Judith Mayne, "Review Essay: Feminist Film Theory and Criticism," *Signs* 11 (Autumn 1985): 83. Subsequent page numbers in parentheses.

9. Claire Johnston, ed., *Notes on Women's Cinema* (London: Society for Education in Film and Television, 1973); Karyn Kay and Gerald Peary, eds., *Women and the Cinema: A Critical Anthology* (New York: Dutton, 1977): and Patricia Erens, ed., *Sexual Stratagems: The World of Women in Film* (New York: Horizon Press, 1979).

10. E. Ann Kaplan, ed. *Women in Film Noir* (London: British Film Institute, 1978).

11. Mary Ann Doane, Patricia Mellencamp, and Linda Williams, eds., *Re-vision: Essays in Feminist Film Criticism*, American Film Institute, Monograph Series, vol. 3 (Los Angeles: University Publications of America / American Film Institute, 1984), 12.

12. Judith Mayne, "Feminist Film Theory and Women at the Movies," *Profession 87* (Modern Language Association Annual), 1987, 17.

13. Doane et al. *Re-vision*, 6.

14. Annette Kuhn, *Women's Pictures: Feminism and Cinema* (London: Routledge and Kegan Paul, 1982).

15. Janet Walker, "Review of *Women's Pictures: Feminism and Cinema* by Annette Kuhn," *Camera Obscura*, no. 12 (Summer 1984): 144–56.

16. For example, "Women's Genres: Melodrama, Soap Opera, and

Theory," *Screen* 25 (January–February 1984): 18–28; and *The Power of the Image: Essays in Representation and Sexuality* (London: Routledge and Kegan Paul, 1985).

17. E. Ann Kaplan, *Women and Film: Both Sides of the Camera* (New York: Methuen, 1983).

18. See especially Diane Waldman and Janet Walker, "Is the Gaze Maternal?: E. Ann Kaplan's *Women and Film: Both Sides of the Camera*," *Camera Obscura,* nos. 13–14 (Spring–Summer 1985): 195–214; Rosemary Betterton, "A Question of Difference: Reviews of *Women and Film* and *Re-vision*," *Screen* 26 (May–August 1985): 102–9; and E. Ann Kaplan, "The Hidden Agenda: *Re-vision: Essays in Feminist Film Criticism*," *Camera Obscura,* nos. 13–14 (Spring–Summer 1985): 235–49.

19. Teresa de Lauretis, *Alice Doesn't: Feminism, Semiotics, Cinema* (Bloomington: Indiana University Press, 1984).

20. Ibid., 6.

21. For example, "Aesthetic and Feminist Theory: Rethinking Women's Cinema," *New German Critique,* no. 34 (Winter 1985): 154–75, as well as "Feminist Studies / Critical Studies: Issues, Terms, and Contexts," in *Feminist Studies / Critical Studies,* ed. de Lauretis (Bloomington: Indiana University Press, 1986), 1–19, and *Technologies of Gender: Essays on Theory, Film, and Fiction* (Bloomington: Indiana University Press, 1987).

22. Mary C. Gentile, *Film Feminisms: Theory and Practice,* Contributions in Women's Studies, no. 56 (Westport, Conn.: Greenwood Press, 1985).

23. Susanne Kappeler, *The Pornography of Representation* (Minneapolis: University of Minnesota Press, 1986).

24. Mary Ann Doane, *The Desire to Desire: The Woman's Film of the 1940s* (Bloomington: Indiana University Press, 1987); Kaja Silverman, *The Acoustic Mirror: The Female Voice in Psychoanalysis and Cinema* (Bloomington: Indiana University Press, 1988); Tania Modleski, *The Women Who Knew Too Much: Hitchcock and Feminist Theory* (New York: Methuen, 1988); and Constance Penley, *The Future of an Illusion: Film, Feminism, and Psychoanalysis* (Minneapolis: University of Minnesota Press, 1989). For an overview of five books published in 1987–88, see Paula Rabinowitz, "Review Essay: Seeing through the Gendered I: Feminist Film Theory," *Feminist Studies* 16 (Spring 1990): 151–69.

25. Tania Modleski, ed., *Studies in Entertainment: Critical Approaches to Mass Culture* (Bloomington: Indiana University Press, 1986); Christine Gledhill, ed., *Home Is Where the Heart Is: Studies in Melodrama and the Woman's Film* (London: BFI Publishing, 1987); E. Deidre Pribram, ed.,

Female Spectators: Looking at Film and Television (New York: Verso, 1988); Constance Penley, ed., *Feminism and Film Theory* (New York: Methuen, 1988); E. Ann Kaplan, ed., *Psychoanalysis and Cinema* (New York: Routledge, 1989); and Lorraine Gammar and Margaret Marshment, eds., *The Female Gaze: Women as Viewers of Popular Culture* (Seattle: Real Comet Press, 1989). For an example of work combining the female gaze, the lesbian subject, and the mother/daughter relationship, see Naomi Scheman, "Missing Mothers / Desiring Daughters: Framing the Sight of Women," *Critical Inquiry* 15 (Autumn 1988): 62–89.

26. Laura Mulvey, "Visual Pleasure and Narrative Cinema," in *Art after Modernism: Rethinking Representation,* ed. Brian Wallis (Boston: David R. Godine, 1984), 361–73; reprinted from *Screen* 16 (Autumn 1975): 6–18. Subsequent page numbers in parentheses. See also an anthology of Mulvey's essays, *Visual and Other Pleasures* (Bloomington: Indiana University Press, 1989).

27. Sam Shepard, *The Tooth of Crime,* in *Sam Shepard: Seven Plays,* intro. Richard Gilman (New York: Bantam Books, 1981), 203. Subsequent page numbers in parentheses.

28. Alice Childress, *Wine in the Wilderness,* in *Plays by and about Women,* ed. Victoria Sullivan and James Hatch (New York: Random House, 1973), 416. Subsequent page numbers in parentheses.

Chapter 6

1. Marilyn Frye, *The Politics of Reality: Essays in Feminist Theory* (Freedom, Calif.: Crossing Press, 1983), 172.

2. Tania Modleski, "Some Functions of Feminist Criticism; or, The Scandal of the Mute Body," *October,* no. 49 (Summer 1989): 13–14.

Bibliography

Plays Discussed

Bowles, Jane. *In the Summer House.* In *My Sister's Hand in Mine: An Expanded Edition of the Collected Works of Jane Bowles,* 203–95. New York: Ecco Press, 1978.

Childress, Alice. *Wine in the Wilderness.* In *Plays by and about Women,* edited by Victoria Sullivan and James Hatch, 379–421. New York: Random House, 1973.

Hellman, Lillian. *Another Part of the Forest.* In *The Collected Plays,* 325–403. Boston: Little, Brown, 1972.

Miller, Arthur. *Death of a Salesman.* New York: Viking, 1949.

O'Neill, Eugene. *The Iceman Cometh.* New York: Random House, 1940; reprint ed., New York: Vintage Books, 1957.

Shepard, Sam. *The Tooth of Crime.* In *Sam Shepard: Seven Plays,* introduction by Richard Gilman, 203–53. New York: Bantam Books, 1981.

Theater Sources

Bamber, Linda. *Comic Women, Tragic Men: A Study of Gender and Genre in Shakespeare.* Palo Alto, Calif.: Stanford University Press, 1981.

Barlow, Judith E., ed. *Plays by American Women: The Early Years.* New York: Avon, 1981.

117

Benmussa Directs. London: John Calder, 1979.

Ben-Zvi, Linda. "Susan Glaspell's Contributions to Contemporary Women Playwrights." In *Feminine Focus*, edited by Enoch Brater, 147–66. New York: Oxford University Press, 1989.

Betsko, Kathleen, and Rachel Koenig. *Interviews with Contemporary Women Playwrights*. New York: Beech Tree Books, 1987.

Bigsby, C. W. E. "Introduction." In *Plays by Susan Glaspell*, edited by C. W. E. Bigsby, 1–31. New York: Cambridge University Press, 1987.

Brater, Enoch, ed. *Feminine Focus: The New Women Playwrights*. New York: Oxford University Press, 1989.

Broe, Mary L. "Bohemia Bumps into Calvin: The Deception of Passivity in Lillian Hellman's Drama." *Southern Quarterly* 19 (Winter 1981): 26–41.

Brown, Janet. *Feminist Drama: Definition and Critical Analysis*. Metuchen, N.J.: Scarecrow Press, 1979.

Brown-Guillory, Elizabeth. *Their Place on Stage: Black Women Playwrights in America*. Westport, Conn.: Greenwood Press, 1988.

Butler, Judith. "Performative Acts and Gender Constitution: An Essay in Phenomenology and Feminist Theory." *Theatre Journal* 40 (December 1988): 519–31.

Callaghan, Dympna. *Women and Gender in Renaissance Tragedy: A Study of King Lear, Othello, the Duchess of Malfi, and the White Devil*. Atlantic Highlands, N.J.: Humanities Press International, 1989.

Carlson, Marvin. *Places of Performance: The Semiotics of Theatre Architecture*. Ithaca, N.Y.: Cornell University Press, 1989.

———. *Theatre Semiotics: Signs of Life*. Bloomington: Indiana University Press, 1990.

Carlson, Susan. "Process and Product: Contemporary British Theatre and Its Communities of Women." *Theatre Research International* 13 (Autumn 1988): 249–63.

———. "Self and Sexuality: Contemporary British Women Playwrights and the Problem of Sexual Identity." *Journal of Dramatic Theory and Criticism* 3 (Spring 1989): 157–78.

Case, Sue-Ellen. "Classic Drag: The Greek Creation of Female Parts." *Theatre Journal* 37 (October 1985): 317–28.

———. *Feminism and Theatre*. New York: Methuen, 1988.

———. "From Split Subject to Split Britches." In *Feminine Focus: The New Women Playwrights*, edited by Enoch Brater, 126–46. New York: Oxford University Press, 1989.

———. "Gender as Play: Simone Benmussa's *The Singular Life of Albert Nobbs*." *Women and Performance* 1 (Winter 1984): 21–24.

———. "Judy Grahn's Gynopoetics: *The Queen of Swords.*" *Studies in the Literary Imagination* 21 (Fall 1988): 47–67.

———. "Re-Viewing Hrotsvit." *Theatre Journal* 35 (December 1983): 533–42.

———. "Toward a Butch-Femme Aesthetic." In *Making a Spectacle: Feminist Essays on Contemporary Women's Theatre,* edited by Lynda Hart, 282–99. Ann Arbor: University of Michigan Press, 1989.

———, ed. *Performing Feminisms: Feminist Critical Theory and Theatre.* Baltimore: Johns Hopkins University Press, 1990.

Case, Sue-Ellen, and Ellen Donkin. "FIT: Germany's First Conference for Women in Theatre." *Women and Performance* 2 (1985): 65–73.

Case, Sue-Ellen, and Jeanie K. Forte. "From Formalism to Feminism." *Theater* 16 (Spring 1985): 62–65.

Chinoy, Helen Krich, and Linda Walsh Jenkins, eds. *Women in American Theatre: Careers, Images, Movements.* New York: Crown, 1981.

———. *Women in American Theatre.* Rev. ed. New York: Theatre Communications Group, 1987.

Clément, Catherine. *Opera; or, The Undoing of Women.* Translated by Betsy Wing. Minneapolis: University of Minnesota Press, 1988.

Cotton, Nancy. *Women Playwrights in England c. 1363–1750.* Lewisburg, Pa.: Bucknell University Press, 1980.

Coven, Brenda. *American Women Dramatists of the Twentieth Century: A Bibliography.* Metuchen, N.J.: Scarecrow Press, 1982.

Curb, Rosemary K. "Re/cognition, Re/presentation, Re/creation in Woman-Conscious Drama: The Seer, the Seen, the Scene, the Obscene." *Theatre Journal* 37 (October 1985): 302–16.

Curtin, Kaier. *"We Can Always Call Them Bulgarians": The Emergence of Lesbians and Gay Men on the American Stage.* Boston: Alyson Publications, 1987.

Cypess, Sandra Messinger. "From Colonial Constructs to Feminist Figures: Re/visions by Mexican Women Dramatists." *Theatre Journal* 41 (December 1989): 492–504.

Dash, Irene G. *Wooing, Wedding, and Power: Women in Shakespeare's Plays.* New York: Columbia University Press, 1981.

Davis, Tracy C. "Questions for a Feminist Methodology in Theatre History." In *Interpreting the Theatrical Past: Essays in the Historiography of Performance,* edited by Thomas Postlewait and Bruce A. McConachie, 59–81. Iowa City: University of Iowa Press, 1989.

Davy, Kate. "Constructing the Spectator: Reception, Context, and Address in Lesbian Performance." *Performing Arts Journal* 10 (Fall 1986): 43–52.

————. "Reading Past the Heterosexual Imperative: *Dress Suits to Hire.*" *TDR* 33 (Spring 1989): 153–70.

De Lauretis, Teresa. "Sexual Indifference and Lesbian Representation." *Theatre Journal* 40 (May 1988): 155–77.

Diamond, Elin. "Brechtian Theory / Feminist Theory: Toward a Gestic Feminist Criticism." *TDR* 32 (Spring 1988): 82–94.

————. *Feminist Stagings: Unmaking Mimesis.* New York.: Routledge, forthcoming.

————. "(In)Visible Bodies in Churchill's Theatre." *Theatre Journal* 40 (May 1988): 188–204.

————. "Mimesis, Mimicry, and the 'True-Real.'" *Modern Drama* 32 (March 1989): 58–72.

————. "Refusing the Romanticism of Identity: Narrative Interventions in Churchill, Benmussa, Duras." *Theatre Journal* 37 (October 1985): 273–86.

Dickerson, Glenda. "The Cult of True Womanhood: Toward a Womanist Attitude in African-American Theatre." *Theatre Journal* 40 (May 1988): 178–87.

Dillon, Millicent. *A Little Original Sin: The Life and Work of Jane Bowles.* New York: Holt, Rinehart, 1981.

Dolan, Jill. "Breaking the Code: Musings on Lesbian Sexuality and the Performer." *Modern Drama* 32 (March 1989): 146–58.

————. "Desire Cloaked in a Trenchcoat." *TDR* 33 (Spring 1989): 59–67.

————. "The Dynamics of Desire: Sexuality and Gender in Pornography and Performance." *Theatre Journal* 39 (May 1987): 156–74.

————. *The Feminist Spectator as Critic.* Ann Arbor, Mich.: UMI Research Press, 1988.

————. "Feminists, Lesbians, and Other Women in Theatre: Thoughts on the Politics of Performance." In *Women in Theatre,* ed. James Redmond, 199–207. Themes in Drama Series, no. 11. New York: Cambridge University Press, 1989.

————. "Gender Impersonation Onstage: Destroying or Maintaining the Mirror of Gender Roles?" *Women and Performance* 2 (1985): 5–11.

————. "In Defense of the Discourse: Materialist Feminism, Postmodernism, Poststructuralism . . . and Theory." *TDR* 33 (Fall 1989): 58–71.

————. "'Lesbian' Subjectivity in Realism: Dragging at the Margins of Structure and Ideology." In *Performing Feminisms: Feminist Critical Theory and Theatre,* edited by Sue-Ellen Case, 40–53. Baltimore: Johns Hopkins University Press, 1990.

————. "The Politics of Feminist Performance." *Theatre Times* 5 (July–August 1986).

Elam, Keir. *The Semiotics of Theatre and Drama*. New York: Methuen, 1980.

Esslin, Martin. *The Field of Drama: How the Signs of Drama Create Meaning on Stage and Screen*. New York: Methuen, 1987.

Féral, Josette. "Performance and Theatricality: The Subject Demystified." *Modern Drama* 25 (March 1982): 170–81.

————. "Writing and Displacement: Women in Theatre." *Modern Drama* 27 (December 1984): 549–63.

Ferris, Lesley. *Acting Women: Images of Women in Theater*. New York: New York University Press, 1989.

Finney, Gail. *Women in Modern Drama: Freud, Feminism, and European Theater at the Turn of the Century*. Ithaca, N.Y.: Cornell University Press, 1989.

Forte, Jeanie. "Realism, Narrative, and the Feminist Playwright—A Problem of Reception." *Modern Drama* 32 (March 1989): 115–27.

————. "Women's Performance Art: Feminism and Postmodernism." *Theatre Journal* 40 (May 1988): 217–35.

France, Rachel, ed. *A Century of Plays by American Women*. New York: Richard Rosen Press, 1979.

French, Marilyn. *Shakespeare's Division of Experience*. New York: Ballantine, 1981.

Gainor, J. Ellen. "A Stage of Her Own: Susan Glaspell's *The Verge* and Women's Dramaturgy." *Journal of American Drama and Theatre* 1 (Spring 1989): 79–99.

Gross, Janice Berkowitz. "Writing across Purposes: The Theatre of Marguerite Duras and Nathalie Sarraute." *Modern Drama* 32 (March 1989): 39–47.

Hart, Lynda. "Introduction: Performing Feminism." In *Making a Spectacle: Feminist Essays on Contemporary Women's Theatre*, edited by Lynda Hart, 1–21. Ann Arbor: University of Michigan Press, 1989.

————, ed. *Making a Spectacle: Feminist Essays on Contemporary Women's Theatre*. Ann Arbor: University of Michigan Press, 1989.

Helms, Lorraine. "Playing the Woman's Part: Feminist Criticism and Shakespearean Performance." *Theatre Journal* 41 (May 1989): 190–200.

Jenkins, Linda Walsh. "Locating the Language of Gender Experience." *Women and Performance* 2 (1984): 5–20.

Jillson, Teresa L. "Working Women's Words and the Conditions of Their

Production(s)." *Journal of Dramatic Theory and Criticism* 2 (Spring 1988): 135–48.

Kelly, Katherine E. "The Queen's Two Bodies: Shakespeare's Boy Actress in Breeches." *Theatre Journal* 42 (March 1990): 81–93.

Keyssar, Helene. *Feminist Theatre: An Introduction to Plays of Contemporary British and American Women*. New York: Grove, 1985.

Kruger, Loren. "The Dis-Play's the Thing: Gender and Public Sphere in Contemporary British Theater." *Theatre Journal* 42 (March 1990): 27–47.

Leavitt, Dinah Luise. *Feminist Theatre Groups*. Jefferson, N.C.: McFarland and Co., 1980.

Lenz, Carolyn R., Gayle Greene, and Carol Thomas Neely. *The Woman's Part: Feminist Criticism of Shakespeare*. Urbana: University of Illinois Press, 1980.

Ley, Ralph. "Beyond 1984: Provocation and Prognosis in Marieluise Fleisser's Play *Purgatory in Ingolstadt.*" *Modern Drama* 31 (September 1988): 340–51.

Malpede, Karen, ed. *Women in Theatre: Compassion and Hope*. New York: Drama Book Publishers, 1983.

McLuskie, Kathleen. *Renaissance Dramatists*. Atlantic HIghlands, N.J.: Humanities Press International, 1989.

Miller, Jeanne-Marie A. "Black Women Playwrights from Grimke to Shange: Selected Synopses of Their Works." In *But Some of Us Are Brave: Black Women's Studies,* edited by Gloria T. Hull, Patricia Bell Scott, and Barbara Smith, 280–96. Old Westbury, N.Y.: Feminist Press, 1982.

Miller, Judith Graves. "Contemporary Women's Voices in French Theatre." *Modern Drama* 32 (March 1989): 5–23.

Moore, Honor, ed. *The New Women's Theatre: Ten Plays by Contemporary American Women*. New York: Random House, 1977.

Moss, Jane. "Women's Theater in France." *Signs* 12 (Spring 1987): 548–67.

Natalle, Elizabeth J. *Feminist Theatre: A Study in Persuasion*. Metuchen, N.J.: Scarecrow Press, 1985.

Novy, Marianne L. *Love's Argument: Gender Relations in Shakespeare*. Chapel Hill: University of North Carolina Press, 1984.

———, ed. *Women's Re-Visions of Shakespeare*. Champaign: University of Illinois Press, 1990.

O'Connor, Patricia W. "Women Playwrights in Contemporary Spain and the Male-Dominated Canon." *Signs* 15 (Winter 1990): 376–90.

Olauson, Judith, *The American Woman Playwright: A View of Criticism and Characterization*. Troy, N.Y.: Whitston, 1981.

Pasquier, Marie-Claire. "Women in the Theatre of Men: What Price Freedom?" In *Women in Culture and Politics*, edited by Judith Friedlander et al., 194–206. Bloomington: Indiana University Press, 1986.

Pavis, Patrice. *Languages of the Stage: Essays in the Semiology of the Theatre*. New York: Performing Arts Journal Publications, 1982.

Perkins, Kathy A. *Black Female Playwrights: Plays before 1950*. Bloomington: Indiana University Press, 1989.

Picard, Anne-Marie. "L'Indiade: Ariane's and Helene's Conjugate Dreams." *Modern Drama* 32 (March 1989): 24–38.

Rackin, Phyllis. "Androgyny, Mimesis, and the Marriage of the Boy Heroine on the English Renaissance Stage." In *Speaking of Gender*, edited by Elaine Showalter, 113–33. New York: Routledge, 1989.

———. "Anti-Historians: Women's Roles in Shakespeare's Histories." *Theatre Journal* 37 (October 1985): 329–44.

Reinelt, Janelle. "Beyond Brecht: Britain's New Feminist Drama." *Theatre Journal* 38 (May 1986): 154–63.

———. "Feminist Theory and the Problem of Performance." *Modern Drama* 32 (March 1989): 48–57.

Reinhardt, Nancy S. "New Directions for Feminist Criticism in Theatre and the Related Arts." In *A Feminist Perspective in the Academy: The Difference It Makes*, edited by Elizabeth Langland and Walter Gove, 25–51. Chicago: University of Chicago Press, 1981.

Rutter, Carol. *Clamorous Voices: Shakespeare's Women Today*. New York: Routledge, 1989.

Savona, Jeannette Laillou, and Ann Wilson. "Introduction." *Modern Drama* 32, "Women in the Theatre" special issue (March 1989): 1–4.

Schlueter, June, ed. *Feminist Rereadings of Modern American Drama*. Madison, N.J.: Fairleigh Dickinson University Press, 1989.

Spencer, Jenny S. "Norman's *'night, Mother*: Psycho-Drama of Female Identity." *Modern Drama* 30 (September 1987): 364–75.

Steadman, Susan M. Flierl. "Feminist Dramatic Criticism: Where We Are Now." *Women and Performance* 4 (1989): 118–48.

Stone, Laurie. "Mother Lode." *Village Voice*, 25 April 1989.

Studies in American Drama, 1945–Present 4, "American Women Playwrights" special issue (1989).

Sullivan, Victoria, and James Hatch, eds., *Plays by and about Women*. New York: Random House, 1973.

Turner, Victor. *The Anthropology of Performance*. New York: Performing Arts Journal Publications, 1988.

———. "Frame, Flow, and Reflection: Ritual and Drama as Public Liminality." In *Performance in Postmodern Culture,* edited by Michel Benamou and Charles Caramello, 35–56. Madison, Wis.: Coda Press, 1977.

———. *From Ritual to Theatre: The Human Seriousness of Play.* New York: Performing Arts Journal Publications, 1982.

Wandor, Michelene. *Carry on, Understudies: Theatre and Sexual Politics.* London: Routledge and Kegan Paul, 1986.

———. *Look Back in Gender: Sexuality and the Family in Post-War British Drama.* New York: Methuen, 1987.

Wilkerson, Margaret B. "Music as Metaphor: New Plays of Black Women." In *Making a Spectacle: Feminist Essays on Contemporary Women's Theatre,* edited by Lynda Hart, 61–75. Ann Arbor: University of Michigan Press, 1989.

———. *"A Raisin in the Sun:* Anniversary of an American Classic." *Theatre Journal* 38 (December 1986): 441–52.

———, ed. *9 Plays by Black Women.* New York: New American Library, 1986.

Wilson, Ann. "History and Hysteria: Writing the Body in *Portrait of Dora* and *Signs of Life." Modern Drama* 32 (March 1989): 73–88.

Women in Theatre. Redmond, James, ed. Themes in Drama Series, no. 11. New York: Cambridge University Press, 1989.

Yarbro-Bejarano, Yvonne. "Chicanas' Experience in Collective Theatre: Ideology and Form." *Women and Performance* 2 (1985): 45–58.

———. "The Female Subject in Chicano Theatre: Sexuality, 'Race,' and Class." *Theatre Journal* 38 (December 1986): 389–407.

Feminism and Fields Other than Theater

Abel, Elizabeth. "Introduction." In *Writing and Sexual Difference,* edited by Elizabeth Abel, 1–7. Chicago: University of Chicago Press, 1982.

———. *Writing and Sexual Difference.* Chicago: University of Chicago Press, 1982.

Alcoff, Linda. "Cultural Feminism Versus Post-Structuralism: The Identity Crisis in Feminist Theory." *Signs* 13 (Spring 1988): 405–36.

Atkinson, Jane Monnig. "Review Essay: Anthropology." *Signs* 8 (Winter 1982): 236–58.

Barrett, Michèle. "Ideology and the Cultural Production of Gender." In *Feminist Criticism and Social Change,* edited by Judith Newton and Deborah Rosenfelt, 65–85. New York: Methuen, 1985.

Baym, Nina. "The Madwoman and Her Languages: Why I Don't Do Feminist Literary Theory." *Tulsa Studies in Women's Literature* 3 (Spring–Fall 1984): 45–59.

Belsey, Catherine. "Constructing the Subject: Deconstructing the Text." In *Feminist Criticism and Social Change,* edited by Judith Newton and Deborah Rosenfelt, 43–64. New York: Methuen, 1985.

Benjamin, Jessica. "A Desire of One's Own: Psychoanalytic Feminism and Intersubjective Space." In *Feminist Studies / Critical Studies,* edited by Teresa de Lauretis, 78–101. Bloomington: Indiana University Press, 1986.

Betterton, Rosemary. "A Question of Difference: Reviews of *Women and Film* and *Re-vision.*" *Screen* 26 (May–August 1985): 102–9.

Bolen, Jean Shinoda. *Goddesses in Everywoman: A New Psychology of Women.* New York: Harper and Row, 1984.

Brennan, Teresa, ed. *Between Feminism and Psychoanalysis.* New York: Routledge, 1989.

Brown, Cheryl L., and Karen Olson, eds. *Feminist Criticism: Essays on Theory, Poetry, and Prose.* Metuchen, N.J.: Scarecrow Press, 1978.

Cameron, Deborah. *Feminism and Linguistic Theory.* New York: St. Martin's Press, 1985.

Chodorow, Nancy. "Being and Doing: A Cross-Cultural Examination of the Socialization of Males and Females." In *Women in Sexist Society: Studies in Power and Powerlessness,* edited by Vivian Gornick and Barbara K. Moran, 259–91. New York: Basic Books, 1971; reprint ed., New York: New American Library, 1972.

———. "Family Structure and Feminine Personality." In *Women, Culture, and Society,* edited by Michelle Zimbalist Rosaldo and Louise Lamphere, 43–66. Stanford, Calif.: Stanford University Press, 1974.

———. *Feminism and Psychoanalytic Theory.* New Haven, Conn.: Yale University Press, 1989.

———. "Mothering, Object-Relations, and the Female Oedipal Configuration." *Feminist Studies* 4 (February 1978): 137–58.

———. "Oedipal Asymmetries and Heterosexual Knots." *Social Problems* 23 (1976): 454–68.

———. *The Reproduction of Mothering: Psychoanalysis and the Sociology of Gender.* Berkeley: University of California Press, 1978.

Christian, Barbara. *Black Feminist Criticism: Perspectives on Black Women Writers.* New York: Pergamon Press, 1985.

———. "The Race for Theory." *Feminist Studies* 14 (Spring 1988): 67–79.

Cixous, Hélène, and Catherine Clément. *The Newly Born Woman*. Minneapolis: University of Minnesota Press, 1986.

Collins, Patricia Hill. "The Social Construction of Black Feminist Thought." *Signs* 14 (Summer 1989): 745–73.

Cornillon, Susan Koppelman, ed. *Images of Women in Fiction: Feminist Perspectives*. Bowling Green, Ohio: Bowling Green University Press, 1972.

Cowie, Elizabeth. "Woman as Sign." *m/f*, no. 1 (1978): 49–63.

De Lauretis, Teresa. "Aesthetic and Feminist Theory: Rethinking Women's Cinema." *New German Critique*, no. 34 (Winter 1985): 154–75.

———. *Alice Doesn't: Feminism, Semiotics, Cinema*. Bloomington: Indiana University Press, 1984.

———. "Eccentric Subjects: Feminist Theory and Historical Consciousness." *Feminist Studies* 16 (Spring 1990): 115–50.

———. "The Essence of the Triangle; or, Taking the Risk of Essentialism Seriously: Feminist Theory in Italy, the U.S., and Britain." *differences* 1 (Summer 1989): 3–37.

———. "Feminist Studies / Critical Studies: Issues, Terms, and Contexts." In *Feminist Studies / Critical Studies,* edited by Teresa de Lauretis, 1–19. Bloomington: Indiana University Press, 1986.

———. *Technologies of Gender: Essays on Theory, Film, and Fiction*. Bloomington: Indiana University Press, 1987.

———, ed. *Feminist Studies / Critical Studies*. Theories of Contemporary Culture Series, vol. 8. Bloomington: Indiana University Press, 1986.

Diamond, Arlyn, and Lee R. Edwards, eds. *The Authority of Experience: Essays in Feminist Criticism*. Boston: University of Massachusetts Press, 1977.

Dinnerstein, Dorothy. *The Mermaid and The Minotaur: Sexual Arrangements and Human Malaise*. New York: Harper and Row, 1976.

Doane, Mary Ann. *The Desire to Desire: The Woman's Film of the 1940s*. Bloomington: Indiana University Press, 1987.

Doane, Mary Ann, Patricia Mellencamp, and Linda Williams, eds. *Re-Vision: Essays in Feminist Film Criticism*. American Film Institute Monograph Series, vol. 3. Los Angeles: University Publications of America / American Film Institute, 1984.

Donaldson, Laura E. "(ex)Changing (wo)Man: Towards a Materialist-Feminist Semiotics." *Cultural Critique*, no. 11 (Winter 1988–89): 5–23.

Donovan, Josephine, ed. *Feminist Literary Criticism: Explorations in Theory*. Lexington: University of Kentucky Press, 1975.

Draine, Betsy. "Review Essay: Refusing the Wisdom of Solomon: Some Recent Feminist Literary Theory." *Signs* 15 (Autumn 1989): 144–70.

DuPlessis, Rachel Blau. *Writing beyond the Ending: Narrative Strategies of Twentieth-Century Women Writers.* Bloomington: Indiana University Press, 1985.

Eagleton, Mary, ed. *Feminist Literary Theory: A Reader.* Oxford, Eng.: Basil Blackwell, 1986.

Echols, Alice. "The New Feminism of Yin and Yang." In *Powers of Desire: The Politics of Sexuality,* edited by Ann Snitow et al., 439–59. New York: Monthly Review Press, 1983.

Ecker, Gisela, ed. *Feminist Aesthetics.* London: Women's Press, 1985.

Eisenstein, Hester, and Alice Jardine, eds. *The Future of Difference.* Boston: G. K. Hall, 1980; reprint ed., New Brunswick, N.J.: Rutgers University Press, 1985.

Farwell, Marilyn R. "Toward a Definition of the Lesbian Literary Imagination." *Signs* 14 (Autumn 1988): 100–118.

Feldstein, Richard, and Judith Roof. *Feminism and Psychoanalysis.* Ithaca, N.Y.: Cornell University Press, 1989.

Ferguson, Ann, Jacquelyn N. Zita, and Pyne Addelson. "On 'Compulsory Heterosexuality and Lesbian Existence': Defining the Issues." In *Feminist Theory: A Critique of Ideology,* edited by Nannerl O. Keohane, Michelle Z. Rosaldo, and Barbara Gelpi, 147–80. Chicago: University of Chicago Press, 1982.

Fetterley, Judith. "Reading about Reading: 'A Jury of Her Peers,' 'The Murders in the Rue Morgue,' and 'The Yellow Wallpaper.'" In *Gender and Reading,* edited by Elizabeth A. Flynn and Patrocinio P. Schweickart, 147–64. Baltimore: Johns Hopkins University Press, 1986.

———. *The Resisting Reader: A Feminist Approach to American Fiction.* Bloomington: Indiana University Press, 1978.

Finke, Laurie. "The Rhetoric of Marginality: Why I Do Feminist Theory." *Tulsa Studies in Women's Literature* 5 (Fall 1986): 251–72.

Flax, Jane. "The Conflict between Nurturance and Autonomy in Mother-Daughter Relationships and Within Feminism." *Feminist Studies* 4 (June 1978): 171–89.

———. "Postmodernism and Gender Relations in Feminist Theory." *Signs* 12 (Summer 1987): 621–43.

Flynn, Elizabeth A., and Patrocinio P. Schweickart, eds. *Gender and Reading: Essays on Readers, Texts, and Contexts.* Baltimore: Johns Hopkins University Press, 1986.

Froula, Christine. "Critical Response II: Pechter's Specter: Milton's Bogey Writ Small; or, Why Is He Afraid of Virginia Woolf?" *Critical Inquiry* 11 (September 1984): 171–78.

———. "When Eve Reads Milton: Undoing the Canonical Economy." *Critical Inquiry* 10 (December 1983): 321–47.

Frye, Marilyn. *The Politics of Reality: Essays in Feminist Theory.* Freedom, Calif.: Crossing Press, 1983.

Gallop, Jane. *The Daughter's Seduction: Feminism and Psychoanalysis.* Ithaca, N.Y.: Cornell University Press, 1982.

———. *Thinking Through the Body.* New York: Columbia University Press, 1988.

Gamman, Lorraine, and Margaret Marshment, eds. *The Female Gaze: Women as Viewers of Popular Culture.* Seattle: Real Comet Press, 1989.

Gardiner, Judith Kegan. "An Interchange on Feminist Criticism: On 'Dancing Through the Minefield.'" *Feminist Studies* 8 (Fall 1982): 629–35.

———. "Mind Mother: Psychoanalysis and Feminism." In *Making a Difference: Feminist Literary Criticism,* edited by Gayle Greene and Coppélia Kahn. New York: Methuen, 1985.

———. "Self Psychology as Feminist Theory." *Signs* 12 (Summer 1987): 761–80.

Garner, Shirley Nelson, Claire Kahane, and Madelon Sprengnether, eds. *The (M)other Tongue: Essays in Feminist Psychoanalytic Interpretation.* Ithaca, N.Y.: Cornell University Press, 1985.

Gentile, Mary C. *Film Feminisms: Theory and Practice.* Contributions in Women's Studies, no. 56. Westport, Conn.: Greenwood Press, 1985.

Gilbert, Sandra M. "Life's Empty Pack: Notes Toward a Literary Daughteronomy." *Critical Inquiry* 11 (March 1985): 355–84.

Gilbert, Sandra M., and Susan Gubar. *The Madwoman in the Attic: The Woman Writer and the Nineteenth-Century Literary Imagination.* New Haven: Yale University Press, 1979.

Gilligan, Carol. *In a Different Voice: Psychological Theory and Women's Development.* Cambridge: Harvard University Press, 1982.

Gledhill, Christine. "Recent Developments in Feminist Criticism." *Quarterly Reveiw of Film Studies* 3 (Fall 1978): 457–93.

———, ed. *Home Is Where the Heart Is: Studies in Melodrama and the Woman's Film.* London: BFI Publishing, 1987.

Greene, Gayle, and Coppélia Kahn, eds. *Making a Difference: Feminist Literary Criticism.* New York: Methuen, 1985.

Gubar, Susan. "Blessings in Disguise: Cross-Dressing as Re-Dressing for Female Modernists." *The Massachusetts Review* 22 (Autumn 1981): 477–508.

Hartsock, Nancy, *Money, Sex, and Power: Toward a Feminist Historical Materialism.* New York: Longman, 1983.

Haskell, Molly. *From Reverence to Rape: The Treatment of Women in the Movies.* Middlesex, Eng.: Penguin Books, 1974.

Hirsch, Marianne. *The Mother/Daughter Plot: Narrative, Psychoanalysis, Feminism.* Bloomington: Indiana University Press, 1989.

———. "Review Essay: Mothers and Daughters." *Signs* 7 (Autumn 1981): 200–222.

hooks, bell. *Feminist Theory: From Margin to Center.* Boston: South End Press, 1984.

Hull, Gloria T., Patricia Bell Scott, and Barbara Smith, eds. *But Some of Us Are Brave: Black Women Studies.* Old Westbury, N.Y.: Feminist Press, 1982.

Humm, Maggie. *Feminist Criticism: Women as Contemporary Critics.* New York: St. Martin's Press, 1986.

Irigaray, Luce. *This Sex Which Is Not One.* Ithaca, N.Y.: Cornell University Press, 1985.

———. *Speculum of the Other Woman.* Ithaca, N.Y.: Cornell University Press, 1985.

Jacobus, Mary, ed. *Women Writing and Writing about Women.* New York: Harper and Row, 1979.

Jaggar, Alison M. *Feminist Politics and Human Nature.* Totowa, N.J.: Rowman and Allanheld, 1983.

Jones, Ann Rosalind. "Inscribing Femininity: French Theories of the Feminine." In *Making a Difference: Feminist Literary Criticism,* edited by Gayle Greene and Coppélia Kahn, 80–112. New York: Methuen, 1985.

———. "Writing the Body: Toward an Understanding of *L'Ecriture Féminine.*" *Feminist Studies* 7 (Summer 1981): 247–63.

Kahn, Coppélia. "The Hand That Rocks the Cradle: Recent Gender Theories and Their Implications." In *The (M)other Tongue: Essays in Feminist Psychoanalytic Interpretation,* edited by Shirley Nelson Garner, Claire Kahane, and Madelen Springnether, 72–88. Ithaca, N.Y.: Cornell University Press, 1985.

Kaplan, E. Ann. "The Hidden Agenda: *Re-Vision: Essays in Feminist Film Criticism.*" *Camera Obscura,* nos. 13–14 (Spring–Summer 1985): 235–49.

———. "Theories of Melodrama: A Feminist Perspective." *Women & Performance* 1 (Spring–Summer 1983): 40–48.

———. *Women and Film: Both Sides of the Camera*. New York: Methuen, 1983.

———, ed. *Psychoanalysis and Cinema*. New York: Routledge, 1989.

———, ed. *Women in Film Noir*. London: British Film Institute, 1978.

Kaplan, Sydney Janet. "Review Essay: Literary Criticism." *Signs* 4 (Spring 1979): 514–27.

———. "Varieties of Feminist Criticism." In *Making a Difference: Feminist Literary Criticism*, edited by Gayle Greene and Coppélia Kahn, 37–58. New York: Methuen, 1985.

Kappeler, Susanne. *The Pornography of Representation*. Minneapolis: University of Minnesota Press, 1986.

Kelley, Joan. *Women, History and Theory: The Essays of Joan Kelly*. Chicago: University of Chicago Press, 1984.

Keohane, Nannerl O., Michelle Z. Rosaldo, and Barbara Gelpi, eds. *Feminist Theory: A Critique of Ideology*. Chicago: University of Chicago Press, 1982.

King, Deborah K. "Multiple Jeopardy, Multiple Consciousness: The Context of a Black Feminist Ideology." *Signs* 14 (Autumn 1988): 42–72.

Kolodny, Annette. "Dancing between Left and Right: Feminism and the Academic Minefield in the 1980s." *Feminist Studies* 14 (Fall 1988): 453–66.

———. "Dancing through the Minefield: Some Observations on the Theory, Practice, and Politics of a Feminist Literary Criticism." *Feminist Studies* 6 (Spring 1980): 1–25.

———. "A Map for Rereading: Gender and the Interpretation of Literary Texts." *New Literary History* 11 (Spring 1980): 451–67.

———. "Review Essay: Literary Criticism." *Signs* 2 (Winter 1976): 404–21.

Kristeva, Julia. *Desire in Language: A Semiotic Approach to Literature and Art*. New York: Columbia University Press, 1980.

———. *The Kristeva Reader*, edited by Toril Moi. New York: Columbia University Press, 1986.

———. *Revolution in Poetic Language*. New York: Columbia University Press, 1984.

Kuhn, Annette. *The Power of the Image: Essays on Representation and Sexuality*. London: Routledge and Kegan Paul, 1985.

———. "Women's Genres: Melodrama, Soap Opera and Theory." *Screen* 25 (January–February 1984): 18–28.

————. *Women's Pictures: Feminism and Cinema*. London: Routledge and Kegan Paul, 1982.

Lerner, Gerda. *The Majority Finds Its Past: Placing Women in History.* New York: Oxford University Press, 1979.

Lorber, Judith, Rose Laub Coser, Alice S. Rossi, and Nancy Chodorow. "On *The Reproduction of Mothering:* A Methodological Debate." *Signs* 6 (Spring 1981): 482–514.

Marcus, Jane. "Storming the Toolshed." In *Feminist Theory: A Critique of Ideology*, edited by Nannerl O. Keohane, Michelle Z. Rosaldo, and Barbara Gelpi, 217–35. Chicago: University of Chicago Press, 1982.

Marks, Elaine, and Isabelle de Courtivron, eds. *New French Feminisms*. New York: Schocken Books, 1981.

Mayne, Judith, "Feminist Film Theory and Women at the Movies." *Profession 87* (Modern Language Association Annual), 1987, 14–19.

————. "Review Essay: Feminist Film Theory and Criticism." *Signs* 11 (Autumn 1985): 81–100.

McConnell-Ginet, Sally, Ruth Borker, and Nelly Furman, eds. *Women and Language in Literature and Society*. New York: Praeger, 1980.

McDowell, Deborah E. "New Directions for Black Feminist Criticism." In *The New Feminist Criticism,* edited by Elaine Showalter, 186–99. New York: Pantheon, 1985.

Meese, Elizabeth A. *Crossing the Double-Cross: The Practice of Feminist Criticism*. Chapel Hill: University of North Carolina Press, 1986.

Miller, Jean Baker. *Toward A New Psychology of Women*. Boston: Beacon Press, 1977.

Miller, Nancy K., ed. *The Poetics of Gender*. Gender and Culture Series. New York: Columbia University Press, 1986.

Millett, Kate. *Sexual Politics*. New York: Doubleday, 1970.

Modleski, Tania. "Some Functions of Feminist Criticism; or, The Scandal of the Mute Body." *October,* no. 49 (Summer 1989): 3–24.

————. *The Women Who Knew Too Much: Hitchcock and Feminist Theory*. New York: Methuen, 1988.

————, ed. *Studies in Entertainment: Critical Approaches to Mass Culture*. Bloomington: Indiana University Press, 1986.

Moi, Toril. *Sexual/Textual Politics: Feminist Literary Theory*. New York: Methuen, 1985.

————, ed. *French Feminist Thought: A Reader*. New York: Basil Blackwell, 1987.

Moore, Henrietta L. *Feminism and Anthropology*. Minneapolis: University of Minnesota Press, 1988.

Mulvey, Laura. "Mulvey on 'Duel in the Sun': Afterthoughts on 'Visual Pleasure and Narrative Cinema' Inspired by 'Duel in the Sun' (King Vidor, 1946)." *Framework,* nos. 15–17 (Summer 1981): 12–15.

———. "Notes on Sirk & Melodrama." *Movie,* no. 25 (Winter 1977–78): 53–56.

———. *Visual and Other Pleasures.* Bloomington: Indiana University Press, 1989.

———. "Visual Pleasure and Narrative Cinema." In *Art after Modernism: Rethinking Representation,* edited by Brian Wallis, 361–73. Boston: David R. Godine, 1984; reprinted from *Screen* 16 (Autumn 1975): 6–18.

Newton, Judith, and Deborah Rosenfelt, eds. *Feminist Criticism and Social Change: Sex, Class, and Race in Literature and Culture.* New York: Methuen, 1985.

Ortner, Sherry B., and Harriet Whitehead, eds. *Sexual Meanings: The Cultural Construction of Gender and Sexuality.* New York: Cambridge University Press, 1981.

Parlee, Mary Brown. "Psychology of Women in the Eighties: Promising Problems." *International Journal of Women's Studies* 8 (March–April 1985): 193–204.

———. "Review Essay: Psychology and Women." *Signs* 5 (Autumn 1979): 121–33.

Pechter, Edward. "Critical Response I: When Pechter Reads Froula Pretending She's Eve Reading Milton; or, New Feminist Is But Old Priest Writ Large." *Critical Inquiry* 11 (September 1984): 163–70.

Penley, Constance. *The Future of an Illusion: Film, Feminism, and Psychoanalysis.* Minneapolis: University of Minnesota Press, 1989.

———, ed. *Feminism and Film Theory.* New York: Methuen, 1988.

Place, Janey, and Julianne Burton. "Feminist Film Criticism." *Movie,* no. 22 (Spring 1976): 53–62.

Pribram, E. Deidre. *Female Spectators: Looking at Film and Television.* New York: Verso, 1988.

Rabinowitz, Paula. "Review Essay: Seeing through the Gendered I: Feminist Film Theory." *Feminist Studies* 16 (Spring 1990): 151–69.

Rainwater, Catherine, and William J. Scheick, eds. *Contemporary American Women Writers: Narrative Strategies.* Lexington: University Press of Kentucky, 1985.

Register, Cheri. "American Feminist Literary Criticism: A Bibliographical Introduction." In *Feminist Literary Criticism: Explorations in Theory,* edited by Josephine Donovan, 1–28. Lexington: University of Kentucky Press, 1975.

———. "Review Essay: Literary Criticism." *Signs* 6 (Winter 1980): 268–82.

Reiter, Rayna, ed. *Toward an Anthropology of Women*. New York: Monthly Review Press, 1975.

Rich, Adrienne. "Compulsory Heterosexuality and Lesbian Existence." *Signs* 5 (Summer 1980): 631–60.

———. *Of Woman Born: Motherhood As Experience and Institution*. New York: Norton, 1976.

———. *On Lies, Secrets, and Silence: Selected Prose, 1966–1978*. New York: Norton, 1979.

Robinson, Lillian S. *Sex, Class, and Culture*. Bloomington: Indiana University Press, 1978.

Rosaldo, Michelle Zimbalist, and Louise Lamphere, eds. *Women, Culture, and Society*. Stanford, Calif.: Stanford University Press, 1974.

Rosen, Marjorie. *Popcorn Venus*. New York: Avon, 1973.

Rubin, Gayle. "The Traffic in Women: Notes on the 'Political Economy' of Sex." In *Toward an Anthropology of Women*, edited by Rayna Reiter, 157–210. New York: Monthly Review Press, 1975.

Russ, Joanna. *How to Suppress Women's Writing*. Austin: University of Texas Press, 1983.

Salvaggio, Ruth. "Theory and Space, Space and Women." *Tulsa Studies in Women's Literature* 7 (Fall 1988): 261–82.

Scheman, Naomi. "Missing Mothers / Desiring Daughters: Framing the Sight of Women." *Critical Inquiry* 15 (Autumn 1988): 62–89.

Sedgwick, Eve Kosofsky. *Between Men: English Literature and Male Homosocial Desire*. New York: Columbia University Press, 1985.

———. "Sexualism and the Citizen of the World: Wycherley, Sterne, and Male Homosocial Desire." *Critical Inquiry* 11 (December 1984): 226–45.

Sheridan, Susan, ed. *Grafts: Feminist Cultural Criticism*. New York: Verso, 1988.

Showalter, Elaine. "Feminist Criticism in the Wilderness." In *The New Feminist Criticism: Essays on Women, Literature, and Theory*, edited by Elaine Showalter, 243–70. New York: Pantheon Books, 1985.

———. "Introduction: The Feminist Critical Revolution." In *The New Feminist Criticism: Essays on Women, Literature, and Theory*, edited by Elaine Showalter, 3–17. New York: Pantheon Books, 1985.

———. *A Literature of Their Own: British Women Novelists from Brontë to Lessing*. Princeton, N.J.: Princeton University Press, 1977.

———. "Review Essay: Literary Criticism." *Signs* 1 (Winter 1975): 435–60.

———. "Towards a Feminist Poetics." In *The New Feminist Criticism: Essays on Women, Literature, and Theory,* edited by Elaine Showalter, 125–43. New York: Pantheon Books, 1985.

———. "Women's Time, Women's Space: Writing the History of Feminist Criticism." *Tulsa Studies in Women's Literature* 3 (Spring–Fall 1984): 29–43.

———, ed. *The New Feminist Criticism: Essays on Women, Literature, and Theory.* New York: Pantheon Books, 1985.

———, ed. *Speaking of Gender.* New York: Routledge, 1989.

Silverman, Kaja. *The Acoustic Mirror: The Female Voice in Psychoanalysis and Cinema.* Bloomington: Indiana University Press, 1988.

———. *The Subject of Semiotics.* New York: Oxford University Press, 1983.

Smith, Barbara. "Toward a Black Feminist Criticism." In *The New Feminist Criticism: Essays on Women, Literature, and Theory,* edited by Elaine Showalter, 168–85. New York: Pantheon, 1985.

Smith, Valerie. "Gender and Afro-Americanist Literary Theory and Criticism." In *Speaking of Gender,* edited by Elaine Showalter, 56–70. New York: Routledge, 1989.

Spelman, Elizabeth V. *Inessential Woman: Problems of Exclusion in Feminist Thought.* Boston: Beacon Press, 1989.

Strathern, Marilyn. "An Awkward Relationship: The Case of Feminism and Anthropology." *Signs* 12 (Winter 1987): 276–92.

Suleiman, Susan, and Inge Crosman, eds. *The Reader in the Text: Essays on Audience and Interpretation.* Princeton University Press, 1980.

Tate, Claudia. "Review Essay: On Black Literary Women and the Evolution of Critical Discourse." *Tulsa Studies in Women's Literature* 5 (Spring 1986): 111–23.

———. "Review Essay: Reshuffling the Deck; or, (Re)Reading Race and Gender in Black Women's Writing." *Tulsa Studies in Women's Literature* 7 (Spring 1988): 119–32.

Todd, Janet. *Feminist Literary History.* New York: Routledge, 1988.

Tompkins, Jane P., ed. *Reader-Response Criticism: From Formalism to Post-Structuralism.* Baltimore: Johns Hopkins University Press, 1980.

Tong, Rosemarie. *Feminist Thought: A Comprehensive Introduction.* Boulder, Colo.: Westview Press, 1989.

Waldman, Diana, and Janet Walker. "Is the Gaze Maternal?: E. Ann Kaplan's *Women and Film: Both Sides of the Camera.*" *Camera Obscura,* nos. 13–14 (Spring–Summer 1985): 195–214.

Walker, Janet. "Review of *Women's Pictures: Feminism and Cinema* by Annette Kuhn." *Camera Obscura,* no. 12 (Summer 1984): 144–56.

Walsh, Mary Roth, ed. *The Psychology of Women: Ongoing Debates.* New Haven: Yale University Press, 1987.

Willis, Susan. "Black Women Writers: Taking a Critical Perspective." In *Making a Difference: Feminist Literary Criticism,* edited by Gayle Greene and Coppélia Kahn, 211–37. New York: Methuen, 1985.

———. "Hélène Cixous's *Portrait de Dora:* The Unseen and the Unscene." *Theatre Journal* 37 (October 1985): 287–301.

Wittig, Monique. "One Is Not Born a Woman." *Feminist Issues* 1 (Winter 1981): 47–54.

———. "The Point of View: Universal or Particular?" *Feminist Issues* 3 (Fall 1983): 63–69.

Women & Therapy: A Feminist Quarterly 6, no. 4 "Race and Gender" (Special issue, Winter 1987).

Zimmerman, Bonnie. "What Has Never Been: An Overview of Lesbian Feminist Criticism." In *Making a Difference: Feminist Literary Criticism,* edited by Gayle Greene and Coppélia Kahn, 177–210. New York: Methuen, 1985.

Index